MEMOIRS OF MARGUERITE DE VALOIS QUEEN OF NAVARRE

MARGUERITE DE VALOIS

Contents

PUBLISHER'S NOTE...7
TRANSLATOR'S PREFACE...8
BOOK 1. 15
LETTER I. 15
LETTER II. 21
LETTER III. 26
LETTER IV. 31
LETTER V. 36
LETTER VI. 40
LETTER VII. 43
LETTER VIII. 46
LETTER IX. 51
LETTER X. 56
LETTER XI. 61
LETTER XII. 65
ETEXT EDITOR'S BOOKMARKS: 71

MEMOIRS OF MARGUERITE DE VALOIS QUEEN OF NAVARRE

BY

MARGUERITE DE VALOIS

PUBLISHER'S NOTE.

The first volume of the Court Memoir Series will, it is confidently anticipated, prove to be of great interest. These Letters first appeared in French, in 1628, just thirteen years after the death of their witty and beautiful authoress, who, whether as the wife for many years of the great Henri of France, or on account of her own charms and accomplishments, has always been the subject of romantic interest.

The letters contain many particulars of her life, together with many anecdotes hitherto unknown or forgotten, told with a saucy vivacity which is charming, and an air vividly recalling the sprightly, arch demeanour, and black, sparkling eyes of the fair Queen of Navarre. She died in 1615, aged sixty-three.

These letters contain the secret history of the Court of France during the seventeen eventful years 1565-82.

The events of the seventeen years referred to are of surpassing interest, including, as they do, the Massacre of St. Bartholomew, the formation of the League, the Peace of Sens, and an account of the religious struggles which agitated that period. They, besides, afford an instructive insight into royal life at the close of the sixteenth century, the modes of travelling then in vogue, the manners and customs of the time, and a picturesque account of the city of Liege and its sovereign bishop.

As has been already stated, these Memoirs first appeared in French in 1628. They were, thirty years later, printed in London in English, and were again there translated and published in 1813.

TRANSLATOR'S PREFACE.

The Memoirs, of which a new translation is now presented to the public, are the undoubted composition of the celebrated princess whose name they bear, the contemporary of our Queen Elizabeth; of equal abilities with her, but of far unequal fortunes. Both Elizabeth and Marguerite had been bred in the school of adversity; both profited by it, but Elizabeth had the fullest opportunity of displaying her acquirements in it. Queen Elizabeth met with trials and difficulties in the early part of her life, and closed a long and successful reign in the happy possession of the good-will and love of her subjects. Queen Marguerite, during her whole life, experienced little else besides mortification and disappointment; she was suspected and hated by both Protestants and Catholics, with the latter of whom, though, she invariably joined in communion, yet was she not in the least inclined to persecute or injure the former. Elizabeth amused herself with a number of suitors, but never submitted to the yoke of matrimony. Marguerite, in compliance with the injunctions of the Queen her mother, and King Charles her brother, married Henri, King of Navarre, afterwards Henri IV. of France, for whom she had no inclination; and this union being followed by a mutual indifference and dislike, she readily consented to dissolve it; soon after which event she saw a princess, more fruitful but less prudent, share the throne of her ancestors, of whom she was the only representative. Elizabeth was polluted with the blood of her cousin, the Queen of Scots, widow of Marguerite's eldest brother. Marguerite saved many Huguenots from the massacre of St. Bartholomew's Day, and, according to Brantome, the life of the King, her husband, whose name was on the list of the proscribed. To close this parallel, Elizabeth began early to govern a kingdom, which she ruled through the course of her long life with severity, yet gloriously, and with success. Marguerite, after the death of the Queen her mother and her brothers, though sole heiress of the

House of Valois, was, by the Salic law, excluded from all pretensions to the Crown of France; and though for the greater part of her life shut up in a castle, surrounded by rocks and mountains, she has not escaped the shafts of obloquy.

The Translator has added some notes, which give an account of such places as are mentioned in the Memoirs, taken from the itineraries of the time, but principally from the "Geographie Universelle" of Vosgien; in which regard is had to the new division of France into departments, as well as to the ancient one of principalities, archbishoprics, bishoprics, generalities, chatellenies, balliages, duchies, seigniories, etc.

In the composition of her Memoirs, Marguerite has evidently adopted the epistolary form, though the work came out of the French editor's hand divided into three (as they are styled) books; these three books, or letters, the Translator has taken the liberty of subdividing into twenty-one, and, at the head of each of them, he has placed a short table of the contents. This is the only liberty he has taken with the original Memoirs, the translation itself being as near as the present improved state of our language could be brought to approach the unpolished strength and masculine vigour of the French of the age of Henri IV.

This translation is styled a new one, because, after the Translator had made some progress in it, he found these Memoirs had already been made English, and printed, in London, in the year 1656, thirty years after the first edition of the French original. This translation has the following title: "The grand Cabinet Counsels unlocked; or, the most faithful Transaction of Court Affairs, and Growth and Continuance of the Civil Wars in France, during the Reigns of Charles the last, Henry III., and Henry IV., commonly called the Great. Most excellently written, in the French Tongue, by Margaret de Valois, Sister to the two first Kings, and Wife of the last. Faithfully translated by Robert Codrington, Master of Arts;" and again as "Memorials of Court Affairs," etc., London, 1658.

The Memoirs of Queen Marguerite contained the secret history of the Court of France during the space of seventeen years, from 1565 to 1582, and they end seven years before Henri III., her brother, fell by the hands of Clement, the monk; consequently, they take in no part of the reign of Henri IV. (as Mr. Codrington has asserted in his title-page), though they relate many particulars of the early part of his life.

Marguerite's Memoirs include likewise the history nearly of the first half of her own life, or until she had reached the twenty-ninth year of her age; and as she died in 1616, at the age of sixty-three years, there remain thirty-four years of her life, of which little is known. In 1598, when she was forty-five years old, her marriage with Henri was dissolved by mutual consent,--she declaring that she had no other wish than to give him content, and preserve the peace of the kingdom; making it her request, according to Brantome, that the King would favour her with his protection, which, as her letter expresses, she hoped to enjoy during the rest of her life. Sully says she stipulated only for an establishment and the payment of her debts, which were granted. After Henri, in 1610, had fallen a victim to the furious fanaticism of the monk Ravaillac, she lived to see the kingdom brought into the greatest confusion by the bad government of the Queen Regent, Marie de Medici, who suffered herself to be directed by an Italian woman she had brought over with her, named Leonora Galligai. This woman marrying a Florentine, called Concini, afterwards made a marshal of France, they jointly ruled the kingdom, and became so unpopular that the marshal was assassinated, and the wife, who had been qualified with the title of Marquise d'Ancre, burnt for a witch. This happened about the time of Marguerite's decease.

It has just before been mentioned how little has been handed down to these times respecting Queen Marguerite's history. The latter part of her life, there is reason to believe, was wholly passed at a considerable distance from Court, in her retirement (so it is called, though it appears to have been rather her prison) at the castle of Usson. This castle, rendered famous by her long residence in it, has been demolished since the year 1634. It was built on a mountain, near a little town of the same name, in that part of France called Auvergne, which now constitutes part of the present Departments of the Upper Loire and Puy-de-Dome, from a river and mountain so named. These Memoirs appear to have been composed in this retreat. Marguerite amused herself likewise, in this solitude, in composing verses, and there are specimens still remaining of her poetry. These compositions she often set to music, and sang them herself, accompanying her voice with the lute, on which she played to perfection. Great part of her time was spent in the perusal of the Bible and books of piety, together with the works of the best authors she could procure. Brantome assures us that Marguerite spoke the Latin tongue with purity and elegance; and it appears, from her Memoirs, that she had read Plutarch with attention.

Marguerite has been said to have given in to the gallantries to which the Court of France was, during her time, but too much addicted; but, though the Translator is obliged to notice it, he is far from being inclined to give any credit to a romance entitled, "Le Divorce Satyrique; ou, les Amours de la Reyne Marguerite de Valois," which is written in the person of her husband, and bears on the title-page these initials: D. R. H. Q. M.; that is to say, "du Roi Henri Quatre, Mari." This work professes to give a relation of Marguerite's conduct during her residence at the castle of Usson; but it contains so many gross absurdities and indecencies that it is undeserving of attention, and appears to have been written by some bitter enemy, who has assumed the character of her husband to traduce her memory.

["Le Divorce Satyrique" is said to have been written by Louise Marguerite de Lorraine, Princesse de Conti, who is likewise the reputed author of "The Amours of Henri IV.," disguised under the name of Alcander. She was the daughter of the Due de Guise, assassinated at Blois in 1588, and was born the year her father died. She married Francois, Prince de Conti, and was considered one of the most ingenious and accomplished persons belonging to the French Court in the age of Louis XIII. She was left a widow in 1614, and died in 1631.]

M. Pierre de Bourdeille, Seigneur de Brantome, better known by the name of Brantome, wrote the Memoirs of his own times. He was brought up in the Court of France, and lived in it during the reigns of Marguerite's father and brothers, dying at the advanced age of eighty or eighty-four years, but in what year is not certainly known.

[The author of the "Tablettes de France," and "Anecdotes des Rois de France," thinks that Marguerite alludes to Brantome's "Anecdotes" in the beginning of her first letter, where she says: "I should commend your work much more were I myself not so much praised in it." (According to the original: "Je louerois davantage votre oeuvre, si elle ne me louoit tant.") If so, these letters were addressed to Brantome, and not to the Baron de la Chataigneraie, as mentioned in the Preface to the French edition. In Letter I. mention is made of Madame de Dampierre, whom Marguerite styles the aunt of the person the letter is addressed to. She was dame d'honneur, or lady of the bedchamber, to the Queen of Henri III., and Brantome, speaking of her, calls her his aunt. Indeed, it is not a matter of any consequence to whom these Memoirs were addressed; it is, however, remarkable that Louis XIV. used the same words to Boileau, after hearing him read his celebrated epistle upon the famous Passage of the Rhine; and yet Louis was no reader, and is not supposed to have adopted them from these Memoirs. The thought is, in reality, fine, but might easily suggest itself to any other. "Cela est beau," said the monarch, "et je vous louerois davantage, si vous m'aviez moins loue." (The poetry is excellent, and I should praise you more had you praised me less.)]

He has given anecdotes of the life of Marguerite, written during her beforementioned retreat, when she was, as he says ("fille unique maintenant restee, de la noble maison de France"), the only survivor of her illustrious house. Brantome praises her excellent beauty in a long string of laboured hyperboles. Ronsard, the Court poet, has done the same in a poem of considerable length, wherein he has exhausted all his wit and fancy. From what they have said, we may collect that Marguerite was graceful in her person and figure, and remarkably happy in her choice of dress and ornaments to set herself off to the most advantage; that her height was above the middle size, her shape easy, with that due proportion of plumpness which gives an appearance of majesty and comeliness. Her eyes were full, black, and sparkling; she had bright, chestnut-coloured hair, and a complexion fresh and blooming. Her skin was delicately white, and her neck admirably well formed; and this so generally admired beauty, the fashion of dress, in her time, admitted of being fully displayed.

Such was Queen Marguerite as she is portrayed, with the greatest luxuriance of colouring, by these authors. To her personal charms were added readiness of wit, ease and gracefulness of speech, and great affability and courtesy of manners. This description of Queen Marguerite cannot be dismissed without observing, if only for the sake of keeping the fashion of the present times with her sex in countenance, that, though she had hair, as has been already described, becoming her, and sufficiently ornamental in itself, yet she occasionally called in the aid of wigs. Brantome's words are: "l'artifice de perruques bien gentiment faconnees."

[Ladies in the days of Ovid wore periwigs. That poet says to Corinna:

"Nunc tibi captivos mittet Germania crines; Culta triumphatae munere gentis eris."

(Wigs shall from captive Germany be sent; 'Tis with such spoils your head you ornament.)

These, we may conclude, were flaxen, that being the prevailing coloured hair of the Germans at this day. The Translator has met with a further account of Marguerite's head-dress, which describes her as wearing a velvet bonnet ornamented with pearls and diamonds, and surmounted with a plume of feathers.]

I shall conclude this Preface with a letter from Marguerite to Brantome; the first, he says, he received from her during her adversity ('son adversite' are his words),--being, as he expresses it, so ambitious ('presomptueux') as to have sent to inquire concerning her health, as she was the daughter and sister of the Kings, his masters. ("D'avoir envoye scavoir de ses nouvelles, mais quoy elle estoit fille et soeur de mes roys.")

The letter here follows: "From the attention and regard you have shown me (which to me appears less strange than it is agreeable), I find you still preserve that attachment you have ever had to my family, in a recollection of these poor remains which have escaped its wreck. Such as I am, you will find me always ready to do you service, since I am so happy as to discover that my fortune has not been able to blot out my name from the memory of my oldest friends, of which number you are one. I have heard that, like me, you have chosen a life of retirement, which I esteem those happy who can enjoy, as God, out of His great mercy, has enabled me to do for these last five years; having placed me, during these times of trouble, in an ark of safety, out of the reach, God be thanked, of storms. If, in my present situation, I am able to serve my friends, and you more especially, I shall be found entirely disposed to it, and with the greatest good-will."

There is such an air of dignified majesty in the foregoing letter, and, at the same time, such a spirit of genuine piety and resignation, that it cannot but give an exalted idea of Marguerite's character, who appears superior to ill-fortune and great even in her distress. If, as I doubt not, the reader thinks the same, I shall not need to make an apology for concluding this Preface with it.

The following Latin verses, or call them, if you please, epigram, are of the composition of Barclay, or Barclaius, author of "Argenis," etc.

ON MARGUERITE DE VALOIS, QUEEN OF NAVARRE.

Dear native land! and you, proud castles! say
(Where grandsire,[1] father,[2] and three brothers[3] lay,
Who each, in turn, the crown imperial wore),
Me will you own, your daughter whom you bore?
Me, once your greatest boast and chiefest pride,
By Bourbon and Lorraine,[4] when sought a bride;
Now widowed wife,[5] a queen without a throne,
Midst rocks and mountains [6] wander I alone.
Nor yet hath Fortune vented all her spite,
But sets one up,[7] who now enjoys my right,
Points to the boy,[8] who henceforth claims the throne
And crown, a son of mine should call his own.
But ah, alas! for me 'tis now too late [9]
To strive 'gainst Fortune and contend with Fate;
Of those I slighted, can I beg relief [10]
No; let me die the victim of my grief.
And can I then be justly said to live?
Dead in estate, do I then yet survive?
Last of the name, I carry to the grave   All the remains the House of Valois have.

1. Francois I.
2. Henri II.
3. Francois II., Charles IX., and Henri III.
4. Henri, King of Navarre, and Henri, Duc de Guise.
5. Alluding to her divorce from Henri IV..
6. The castle of Usson
7. Marie de' Medici, whom Henri married after his divorce from Marguerite.
8. Louis XIII., the son of Henri and his queen, Marie de' Medici.
9. Alluding to the differences betwixt Marguerite and Henri, her husband.
10. This is said with allusion to the supposition that she was rather inclined to favour the suit of the Due de Guise and reject Henri for a husband.

BOOK 1.
LETTER I.

Introduction.--Anecdotes of Marguerite's Infancy.--Endeavours Used to Convert Her to the New Religion.--She Is Confirmed in Catholicism.--The Court on a Progress.--A Grand Festivity Suddenly Interrupted.--The Confusion in Consequence.

I should commend your work much more were I myself less praised in it; but I am unwilling to do so, lest my praises should seem rather the effect of self-love than to be founded on reason and justice. I am fearful that, like Themistocles, I should appear to admire their eloquence the most who are most forward to praise me. It is the usual frailty of our sex to be fond of flattery. I blame this in other women, and should wish not to be chargeable with it myself. Yet I confess that I take a pride in being painted by the hand of so able a master, however flattering the likeness may be. If I ever were possessed of the graces you have assigned to me, trouble and vexation render them no longer visible, and have even effaced them from my own recollection. So that I view myself in your Memoirs, and say, with old Madame de Rendan, who, not having consulted her glass since her husband's death, on seeing her own face in the mirror of another lady, exclaimed, "Who is this?" Whatever my friends tell me when they see me now, I am inclined to think proceeds from the partiality of their affection. I am sure that you yourself, when you consider more impartially what you have said, will be induced to believe, according to these lines of Du Bellay:

"C'est chercher Rome en Rome, Et rien de Rome en Rome ne trouver."

('Tis to seek Rome, in Rome to go, And Rome herself at Rome not know.)

But as we read with pleasure the history of the Siege of Troy, the magnificence of Athens, and other splendid cities, which once flourished, but are now so entirely destroyed that scarcely the spot whereon they stood can be traced, so you please yourself with describing these excellences of beauty which are no more, and which will be discoverable only in your writings.

If you had taken upon you to contrast Nature and Fortune, you could not have chosen a happier theme upon which to descant, for both have made a trial of their strength on the subject of your Memoirs. What Nature did, you had the evidence of your own eyes to vouch for, but what was done by Fortune, you know only from hearsay; and hearsay, I need not tell you, is liable to be influenced by ignorance or malice, and, therefore, is not to be depended on. You will for that reason, I make no doubt, be pleased to receive these Memoirs from the hand which is most interested in the truth of them.

I have been induced to undertake writing my Memoirs the more from five or six observations which I have had occasion to make upon your work, as you appear to have been misinformed respecting certain particulars. For example, in that part where mention is made of Pau, and of my journey in France; likewise where you speak of the late Marechal de Biron, of Agen, and of the sally of the Marquis de Camillac from that place.

These Memoirs might merit the honourable name of history from the truths contained in them, as I shall prefer truth to embellishment. In fact, to embellish my story I have neither leisure nor ability; I shall, therefore, do no more than give a simple narration of events. They are the labours of my evenings, and will come to you an unformed mass, to receive its shape from your hands, or as a chaos on which you have already thrown light. Mine is a history most assuredly worthy to come from a man of honour, one who is a true Frenchman, born of illustrious parents, brought up in the Court of the Kings my father and brothers, allied in blood and friendship to the most virtuous and accomplished women of our times, of which society I have had the good fortune to be the bond of union.

I shall begin these Memoirs in the reign of Charles IX., and set out with the first remarkable event of my life which fell within my remembrance. Herein I follow the example of geographical writers, who, having described the places within their knowledge, tell you that all beyond them are sandy deserts, countries without inhabitants, or seas never navigated. Thus I might say that all prior to the commencement of these Memoirs was the barrenness of my infancy, when we can only be said to vegetate like plants, or live, like brutes, according to instinct, and not as human creatures, guided by reason. To those who had the direction of my earliest years I leave the task of relating the transactions of my infancy, if they find them as worthy of being recorded as the infantine exploits of Themistocles and Alexander,--the one exposing himself to be trampled on by the horses of a charioteer, who would not stop them when requested to do so, and the other refusing to run a race unless kings were to enter the contest against him. Amongst such memorable things might be related the answer I made the King my father, a short time before the fatal accident which deprived France of peace, and our family of its chief glory. I was then about four or five years of age, when the King, placing me on his knee, entered familiarly into chat with me. There were, in the same room, playing and diverting themselves, the Prince de Joinville, since the great and unfortunate Duc de Guise, and the Marquis de Beaupreau, son of the Prince de la Roche-sur-Yon, who died in his fourteenth year, and by whose death his country lost a youth of most promising talents. Amongst other discourse, the King asked which of the two Princes that were before me I liked best. I replied, "The Marquis." The King said, "Why so? He is not the handsomest." The Prince de Joinville was fair, with light-coloured hair, and the Marquis de Beaupreau brown, with dark hair. I answered, "Because he is the best behaved; whilst the Prince is always making mischief, and will be master over everybody."

This was a presage of what we have seen happen since, when the whole Court was infected with heresy, about the time of the Conference of Poissy. It was with great difficulty that I resisted and preserved myself from a change of religion at that time. Many ladies and lords belonging to Court strove to convert me to Huguenotism. The Duc d'Anjou, since King Henri III. of France, then in his infancy, had been prevailed on to change his religion, and he often snatched my "Hours" out of my hand, and flung them into the fire, giving me Psalm Books and books of Huguenot prayers, insisting on my using them. I took the first opportunity to give them up to my governess, Madame de Curton, whom God, out of his mercy to me, caused to continue steadfast in the Catholic religion. She frequently took me to that pious, good man, the Cardinal de Tournon, who gave me good advice, and strengthened me in a perseverance in my religion, furnishing me with books and chaplets of beads in the room of those my brother Anjou took from me and burnt.

Many of my brother's most intimate friends had resolved on my ruin, and rated me severely upon my refusal to change, saying it proceeded from a childish obstinacy; that if I had the least understanding, and would listen, like other discreet persons, to the sermons that were preached, I should abjure my uncharitable bigotry; but I was, said they, as foolish as my governess. My brother Anjou added threats, and said the Queen my mother would give orders that I should be whipped. But this he said of his own head, for the Queen my mother did not, at that time, know of the errors he had embraced. As soon as it came to her knowledge, she took him to task, and severely reprimanded his governors, insisting upon their correcting him, and instructing him in the holy and ancient religion of his forefathers, from which she herself never swerved. When he used those menaces, as I have before related, I was a child seven or eight years old, and at that tender age would reply to him, "Well, get me whipped if you can; I will suffer whipping, and even death, rather than be damned."

I could furnish you with many other replies of the like kind, which gave proof of the early ripeness of my judgment and my courage; but I shall not trouble myself with such researches, choosing rather to begin these Memoirs at the time when I resided constantly with the Queen my mother.

Immediately after the Conference of Poissy, the civil wars commenced, and my brother Alencon and myself, on account of our youth, were sent to Amboise, whither all the ladies of the country repaired to us.

With them came your aunt, Madame de Dampierre, who entered into a firm friendship with me, which was never interrupted until her death broke it off. There was likewise your cousin, the Duchesse de Rais, who had the good fortune to hear there of the death of her brute of a husband, killed at the battle of Dreux. The husband I mean was the first she had, named M. d'Annebaut, who was unworthy to have for a wife so accomplished and charming a woman as your cousin. She and I were not then so intimate friends as we have become since, and shall ever remain. The reason was that, though older than I, she was yet young, and young girls seldom take much notice of children, whereas your aunt was of an age when women admire their innocence and engaging simplicity.

I remained at Amboise until the Queen my mother was ready to set out on her grand progress, at which time she sent for me to come to her Court, which I did not quit afterwards.

Of this progress I will not undertake to give you a description, being still so young that, though the whole is within my recollection, yet the particular passages of it appear to me but as a dream, and are now lost. I leave this task to others, of riper years, as you were yourself. You can well remember the magnificence that was displayed everywhere, particularly at the baptism of my nephew, the Duc de Lorraine, at Bar-le-Duc; at the meeting of M. and Madame de Savoy, in the city of Lyons; the interview at Bayonne betwixt my sister, the Queen of Spain, the Queen my mother, and King Charles my brother. In your account of this interview you would not forget to make mention of the noble entertainment given by the Queen my mother, on an island, with the grand dances, and the form of the salon, which seemed appropriated by nature for such a purpose, it being a large meadow in the middle of the island, in the shape of an oval, surrounded on every aide by tall spreading trees. In this meadow the Queen my mother had disposed a circle of niches, each of them large enough to contain a table of twelve covers. At one end a platform was raised, ascended by four steps formed of turf. Here their Majesties were seated at a table under a lofty canopy. The tables were all served by troops of shepherdesses dressed in cloth of gold and satin, after the fashion of the different provinces of France. These shepherdesses, during the passage of the superb boats from Bayonne to the island, were placed in separate bands, in a meadow on each side of the causeway, raised with turf; and whilst their Majesties and the company were passing through the great salon, they danced. On their passage by water, the barges were followed by other boats, having on board vocal and instrumental musicians, habited like Nereids, singing and playing the whole time. After landing, the shepherdesses I have mentioned before received the company in separate troops, with songs and dances, after the fashion and accompanied by the music of the provinces they represented,--the Poitevins playing on bagpipes; the Provencales on the viol and cymbal; the Burgundians and Champagners on the hautboy, bass viol, and tambourine; in like manner the Bretons and other provincialists. After the collation was served and the feast at an end, a large troop of musicians, habited like satyrs, was seen to come out of the opening of a rock, well lighted up, whilst nymphs were descending from the top in rich habits, who, as they came down, formed into a grand dance, when, lo! fortune no longer favouring this brilliant festival, a sudden storm of rain came on, and all were glad to get off in the boats and make for town as fast as they could. The confusion in consequence of this precipitate retreat afforded as much matter to laugh at the next day as the splendour of the entertainment had excited admiration. In short, the festivity of this day was not, forgotten, on one account or the other, amidst the variety of the like nature which succeeded it in the course of this progress.

LETTER II.

Message from the Duc d'Anjou, Afterwards Henri III., to King Charles His Brother and the Queen-mother.--Her Fondness for Her Children.--Their Interview.--Anjou's Eloquent Harangue.--The Queen-mother's Character. Discourse of the Duc d'Anjou with Marguerite.--She Discovers Her Own Importance.--Engages to Serve Her Brother Anjou.--Is in High Favour with the Queenmother.

At the time my magnanimous brother Charles reigned over France, and some few years after our return from the grand progress mentioned in my last letter, the Huguenots having renewed the war, a gentleman, despatched from my brother Anjou (afterwards Henri III. of France), came to Paris to inform the King and the Queen my mother that the Huguenot army was reduced to such an extremity that he hoped in a few days to force them to give him battle. He added his earnest wish for the honour of seeing them at Tours before that happened, so that, in case Fortune, envying him the glory he had already achieved at so early an age, should, on the so much looked-for day, after the good service he had done his religion and his King, crown the victory with his death, he might not have cause to regret leaving this world without the satisfaction of receiving their approbation of his conduct from their own mouths, a satisfaction which would be more valuable, in his opinion, than the trophies he had gained by his two former victories.

I leave to your own imagination to suggest to you the impression which such a message from a dearly beloved son made on the mind of a mother who doted on all her children, and was always ready to sacrifice her own repose, nay, even her life, for their happiness.

She resolved immediately to set off and take the King with her. She had, besides myself, her usual small company of female attendants, together with Mesdames de Rais and de Sauves. She flew on the wings of maternal affection, and reached Tours in three days and a half. A journey from Paris, made with such precipitation, was not unattended with accidents and some inconveniences, of a nature to occasion much mirth and laughter. The poor Cardinal de Bourbon, who never quitted her, and whose temper of mind, strength of body, and habits of life were ill suited to encounter privations and hardships, suffered greatly from this rapid journey.

We found my brother Anjou at Plessis-les-Tours, with the principal officers of his army, who were the flower of the princes and nobles of France. In their presence he delivered a harangue to the King, giving a detail of his conduct in the execution of his charge, beginning from the time he left the Court. His discourse was framed with so much eloquence, and spoken so gracefully, that it was admired by all present. It appeared matter of astonishment that a youth of sixteen should reason with all the gravity and powers of an orator of ripe years. The comeliness of his person, which at all times pleads powerfully in favour of a speaker, was in him set off by the laurels obtained in two victories. In short, it was difficult to say which most contributed to make him the admiration of all his hearers.

It is equally as impossible for me to describe in words the feelings of my mother on this occasion, who loved him above all her children, as it was for the painter to represent on canvas the grief of Iphigenia's father. Such an overflow of joy would have been discoverable in the looks and actions of any other woman, but she had her passions so much under the control of prudence and discretion that there was nothing to be perceived in her countenance, or gathered from her words, of what she felt inwardly in her mind. She was, indeed, a perfect mistress of herself, and regulated her discourse and her actions by the rules of wisdom and sound policy, showing that a person of discretion does upon all occasions only what is proper to be done. She did not amuse herself on this occasion with listening to the praises which issued from every mouth, and sanction them with her own approbation; but, selecting the chief points in the speech relative to the future conduct of the war, she laid them before the Princes and great lords, to be deliberated upon, in order to settle a plan of operations.

To arrange such a plan a delay of some days was requisite. During this interval, the Queen my mother walking in the park with some of the Princes, my brother

Anjou begged me to take a turn or two with him in a retired walk. He then addressed me in the following words: "Dear sister, the nearness of blood, as well as our having been brought up together, naturally, as they ought, attach us to each other. You must already have discovered the partiality I have had for you above my brothers, and I think that I have perceived the same in you for me. We have been hitherto led to this by nature, without deriving any other advantage from it than the sole pleasure of conversing together. So far might be well enough for our childhood, but now we are no longer children. You know the high situation in which, by the favour of God and our good mother the Queen, I am here placed. You may be assured that, as you are the person in the world whom I love and esteem the most, you will always be a partaker of my advancement. I know you are not wanting in wit and discretion, and I am sensible you have it in your power to do me service with the Queen our mother, and preserve me in my present employments. It is a great point obtained for me, always to stand well in her favour. I am fearful that my absence may be prejudicial to that purpose, and I must necessarily be at a distance from Court. Whilst I am away, the King my brother is with her, and has it in his power to insinuate himself into her good graces. This I fear, in the end, may be of disservice to me. The King my brother is growing older every day. He does not want for courage, and, though he now diverts himself with hunting, he may grow ambitious, and choose rather to chase men than beasts; in such a case I must resign to him my commission as his lieutenant. This would prove the greatest mortification that could happen to me, and I would even prefer death to it. Under such an apprehension I have considered of the means of prevention, and see none so feasible as having a confidential person about the Queen my mother, who shall always be ready to espouse and support my cause. I know no one so proper for that purpose as yourself, who will be, I doubt not, as attentive to my interest as I should be myself. You have wit, discretion, and fidelity, which are all that are wanting, provided you will be so kind as to undertake such a good office. In that case I shall have only to beg of you not to neglect attending her morning and evening, to be the first with her and the last to leave her. This will induce her to repose a confidence and open her mind to you.

"To make her the more ready to do this, I shall take every opportunity, to commend your good sense and understanding, and to tell her that I shall take it kind in her to leave off treating you as a child, which, I shall say, will contribute to her own comfort and satisfaction. I am well convinced that she will listen to my advice. Do you speak to her with the same confidence as you do to me, and be assured that she will approve of it. It will conduce to your own happiness to obtain her favour. You may do yourself service whilst you are labouring for my interest; and you may rest satisfied that, after God, I shall think I owe all the good fortune which may befall me to yourself."

This was entirely a new kind of language to me. I had hitherto thought of nothing but amusements, of dancing, hunting, and the like diversions; nay, I had never yet discovered any inclination of setting myself off to advantage by dress, and exciting an admiration of my person and figure. I had no ambition of any kind, and had been so strictly brought up under the Queen my mother that I scarcely durst speak before her; and if she chanced to turn her eyes towards me I trembled, for fear that I had done something to displease her. At the conclusion of my brother's harangue, I was half inclined to reply to him in the words of Moses, when he was spoken to from the burning bush: "Who am I, that I should go unto Pharaoh? Send, I pray thee, by the hand of him whom thou wilt send."

However, his words inspired me with resolution and powers I did not think myself possessed of before. I had naturally a degree of courage, and, as soon as I recovered from my astonishment, I found I was quite an altered person. His address pleased me, and wrought in me a confidence in myself; and I found I was become of more consequence than I had ever conceived I had been. Accordingly, I replied to him thus: "Brother, if God grant me the power of speaking to the Queen our mother as I have the will to do, nothing can be wanting for your service, and you may expect to derive all the good you hope from it, and from my solicitude and attention for your interest. With respect to my undertaking such a matter for you, you will soon perceive that I shall sacrifice all the pleasures in this world to my watchfulness for your service. You may perfectly rely on me, as there is no one that honours or regards you more than I do. Be well assured that I shall act for you with the Queen my mother as zealously as you would for yourself."

These sentiments were more strongly impressed upon my mind than the words I made use of were capable of conveying an idea of. This will appear more fully in my following letters.

As soon as we were returned from walking, the Queen my mother retired with me into her closet, and addressed the following words to me: "Your brother has been relating the conversation you have had together; he considers you no longer as a child, neither shall I. It will be a great comfort to me to converse with you as I would with your brother. For the future you will freely speak your mind, and have no apprehensions of taking too great a liberty, for it is what I wish." These words gave me a pleasure then which I am now unable to express. I felt a satisfaction and a joy which nothing before had ever caused me to feel. I now considered the pastimes of my childhood as vain amusements. I shunned the society of my former companions of the same age. I disliked dancing and hunting, which I thought beneath my attention. I strictly complied with her agreeable injunction, and never missed being with her at her rising in the morning and going to rest at night. She did me the honour, sometimes, to hold me in conversation for two and three hours at a time. God was so gracious with me that I gave her great satisfaction; and she thought she could not sufficiently praise me to those ladies who were about her. I spoke of my brother's affairs to her, and he was constantly apprised by me of her sentiments and opinion; so that he had every reason to suppose I was firmly attached to his interest.

LETTER III.

Le Guast.--His Character.--Anjou Affects to Be Jealous of the Guises.--Dissuades the Queen-mother from Reposing Confidence in Marguerite.--She Loses the Favour of the Queen-mother and Falls Sick.--Anjou's Hypocrisy.--He Introduces De Guise into Marguerite's Sick Chamber.--Marguerite Demanded in Marriage by the King of Portugal.--Made Uneasy on That Account.--Contrives to Relieve Herself.--The Match with Portugal Broken off.

I continued to pass my time with the Queen my mother, greatly to my satisfaction, until after the battle of Moncontour. By the same despatch that brought the news of this victory to the Court, my brother, who was ever desirous to be near the Queen my mother, wrote her word that he was about to lay siege to St. Jean d'Angely, and that it would be necessary that the King should be present whilst it was going on.

She, more anxious to see him than he could be to have her near him, hastened to set out on the journey, taking me with her, and her customary train of attendants. I likewise experienced great joy upon the occasion, having no suspicion that any mischief awaited me. I was still young and without experience, and I thought the happiness I enjoyed was always to continue; but the malice of Fortune prepared for me at this interview a reverse that I little expected, after the fidelity with which I had discharged the trust my brother had reposed in me.

Soon after our last meeting, it seems, my brother Anjou had taken Le Guast to be near his person, who had ingratiated himself so far into his favour and confidence that he saw only with his eyes, and spoke but as he dictated. This evil-disposed man, whose whole life was one continued scene of wickedness, had perverted his mind and filled it with maxims of the most atrocious nature. He advised him to have no regard but for his own interest; neither to love nor put trust in any one; and not to promote the views or advantage of either brother or sister. These and other maxims of the like nature, drawn from the school of Machiavelli, he was continually suggesting to him. He had so frequently inculcated them that they were strongly impressed on his mind, insomuch that, upon our arrival, when, after the first compliments, my mother began to open in my praise and express the attachment I had discovered for him, this was his reply, which he delivered with the utmost coldness:

"He was well pleased," he said, "to have succeeded in the request he had made to me; but that prudence directed us not to continue to make use of the same expedients, for what was profitable at one time might not be so at another." She asked him why he made that observation. This question afforded the opportunity he wished for, of relating a story he had fabricated, purposely to ruin me with her.

He began with observing to her that I was grown very handsome, and that M. de Guise wished to marry me; that his uncles, too, were very desirous of such a match; and, if I should entertain a like passion for him, there would be danger of my discovering to him all she said to me; that she well knew the ambition of that house, and how ready they were, on all occasions, to circumvent ours. It would, therefore, be proper that she should not, for the future, communicate any matter of State to me, but, by degrees, withdraw her confidence.

I discovered the evil effects proceeding from this pernicious advice on the very same evening. I remarked an unwillingness on her part to speak to me before my brother; and, as soon as she entered into discourse with him, she commanded me to go to bed. This command she repeated two or three times. I quitted her closet, and left them together in conversation; but, as soon as he was gone, I returned and entreated her to let me know if I had been so unhappy as to have done anything, through ignorance, which had given her offence. She was at first inclined to dissemble with me; but at length she said to me thus: "Daughter, your brother is prudent and cautious; you ought not to be displeased with him for what he does, and you must believe what I shall tell you is right and proper." She then related the conversation she had with my brother, as I have just written it; and she then ordered me never to speak to her in my brother's presence.

These words were like so many daggers plunged into my breast. In my disgrace, I experienced as much grief as I had before joy on being received into her favour and confidence. I did not omit to say everything to convince her of my entire ignorance of what my brother had told her. I said it was a matter I had never heard mentioned before; and that, had I known it, I should certainly have made her immediately acquainted with it. All I said was to no purpose; my brother's words had made the first impression; they were constantly present in her mind, and outweighed probability and truth. When I discovered this, I told her that I felt less uneasiness at being deprived of my happiness than I did joy when I had acquired it; for my brother had taken it from me, as he had given it. He had given it without reason; he had taken it away without cause. He had praised me for discretion and prudence when I did not merit it, and he suspected my fidelity on grounds wholly imaginary and fictitious. I concluded with assuring her that I should never forget my brother's behaviour on this occasion.

Hereupon she flew into a passion and commanded me not to make the least show of resentment at his behaviour. From that hour she gradually withdrew her favour from me. Her son became the god of her idolatry, at the shrine of whose will she sacrificed everything.

The grief which I inwardly felt was very great and overpowered all my faculties, until it wrought so far on my constitution as to contribute to my receiving the infection which then prevailed in the army. A few days after I fell sick of a raging fever, attended with purple spots, a malady which carried off numbers, and, amongst the rest, the two principal physicians belonging to the King and Queen, Chappelain and Castelan. Indeed, few got over the disorder after being attacked with it.

In this extremity the Queen my mother, who partly guessed the cause of my illness, omitted nothing that might serve to remove it; and, without fear of consequences, visited me frequently. Her goodness contributed much to my recovery; but my brother's hypocrisy was sufficient to destroy all the benefit I received from her attention, after having been guilty of so treacherous a proceeding. After he had proved so ungrateful to me, he came and sat at the foot of my bed from morning to night, and appeared as anxiously attentive as if we had been the most perfect friends. My mouth was shut up by the command I had received from the Queen our mother, so that I only answered his dissembled concern with sighs, like Burrus in the presence of Nero, when he was dying by the poison administered by the hands of that tyrant. The sighs, however, which I vented in my brother's presence, might convince him that I attributed my sickness rather to his ill offices than to the prevailing contagion.

God had mercy on me, and supported me through this dangerous illness. After I had kept my bed a fortnight, the army changed its quarters, and I was conveyed away with it in a litter. At the end of each day's march, I found King Charles at the door of my quarters, ready, with the rest of the good gentlemen belonging to the Court, to carry my litter up to my bedside. In this manner I came to Angers from St. Jean d'Angely, sick in body, but more sick in mind. Here, to my misfortune, M. de Guise and his uncles had arrived before me. This was a circumstance which gave my good brother great pleasure, as it afforded a colourable appearance to his story. I soon discovered the advantage my brother would make of it to increase my already too great mortification; for he came daily to see me, and as constantly brought M. de Guise into my chamber with him. He pretended the sincerest regard for De Guise, and, to make him believe it, would take frequent opportunities of embracing him, crying out at the same time, "would to God you were my brother!" This he often put in practice before me, which M. de Guise seemed not to comprehend; but I, who knew his malicious designs, lost all patience, yet did not dare to reproach him with his hypocrisy.

As soon as I was recovered, a treaty was set on foot for a marriage betwixt the King of Portugal and me, an ambassador having been sent for that purpose. The Queen my mother commanded me to prepare to give the ambassador an audience; which I did accordingly. My brother had made her believe that I was averse to this marriage; accordingly, she took me to task upon it, and questioned me on the subject, expecting she should find some cause to be angry with me. I told her my will had always been guided by her own, and that whatever she thought right for me to do, I should do it. She answered me, angrily, according as she had been wrought upon, that I did not speak the sentiments of my heart, for she well knew that the Cardinal de Lorraine had persuaded me into a promise of having his nephew. I begged her to forward this match with the King of Portugal, and I would convince her of my obedience to her commands. Every day some new matter was reported to incense her against me. All these were machinations worked up by the mind of

Le Guast. In short, I was constantly receiving some fresh mortification, so that I hardly passed a day in quiet. On one side, the King of Spain was using his utmost endeavours to break off the match with Portugal, and M. de Guise, continuing at Court, furnished grounds for persecuting me on the other. Still, not a single person of the Guises ever mentioned a word to me on the subject; and it was well known that, for more than a twelvemonth, M. de Guise had been paying his addresses to the Princesse de Porcian; but the slow progress made in bringing this match to a conclusion was said to be owing to his designs upon me.

As soon as I made this discovery I resolved to write to my sister, Madame de Lorraine, who had a great influence in the House of Porcian, begging her to use her endeavours to withdraw M. de Guise from Court, and make him conclude his match with the Princess, laying open to her the plot which had been concerted to ruin the Guises and me. She readily saw through it, came immediately to Court, and concluded the match, which delivered me from the aspersions cast on my character, and convinced the Queen my mother that what I had told her was the real truth. This at the same time stopped the mouths of my enemies and gave me some repose.

At length the King of Spain, unwilling that the King of Portugal should marry out of his family, broke off the treaty which had been entered upon for my marriage with him.

LETTER IV.

Death of the Queen of Navarre--Marguerite's Marriage with Her Son, the King of Navarre, Afterwards Henri IV. of France.--The Preparations for That Solemnisation Described.--The Circumstances Which Led to the Massacre of the Huguenots on St. Bartholomew's Day.

Some short time after this a marriage was projected betwixt the Prince of Navarre, now our renowned King Henri IV., and me.

The Queen my mother, as she sat at table, discoursed for a long time upon the subject with M. de Meru, the House of Montmorency having first proposed the match. After the Queen had risen from table, he told me she had commanded him to mention it to me. I replied that it was quite unnecessary, as I had no will but her own; however, I should wish she would be pleased to remember that I was a Catholic, and that I should dislike to marry any one of a contrary persuasion.

Soon after this the Queen sent for me to attend her in her closet. She there informed me that the Montmorencys had proposed this match to her, and that she was desirous to learn my sentiments upon it.

I answered that my choice was governed by her pleasure, and that I only begged her not to forget that I was a good Catholic.

This treaty was in negotiation for some time after this conversation, and was not finally settled until the arrival of the Queen of Navarre, his mother, at Court, where she died soon after.

Whilst the Queen of Navarre lay on her death-bed, a circumstance happened of so whimsical a nature that, though not of consequence to merit a place in the history, it may very well deserve to be related by me to you. Madame de Nevers, whose oddities you well know, attended the Cardinal de Bourbon, Madame de

Guise, the Princesse de Conde, her sisters, and myself to the late Queen of Navarre's apartments, whither we all went to pay those last duties which her rank and our nearness of blood demanded of us. We found the Queen in bed with her curtains undrawn, the chamber not disposed with the pomp and ceremonies of our religion, but after the simple manner of the Huguenots; that is to say, there were no priests, no cross, nor any holy water. We kept ourselves at some distance from the bed, but Madame de Nevers, whom you know the Queen hated more than any woman besides, and which she had shown both in speech and by actions,--Madame de Nevers, I say, approached the bedside, and, to the great astonishment of all present, who well knew the enmity subsisting betwixt them, took the Queen's hand, with many low curtseys, and kissed it; after which, making another curtsey to the very ground, she retired and rejoined us.

A few months after the Queen's death, the Prince of Navarre, or rather, as he was then styled, the King, came to Paris in deep mourning, attended by eight hundred gentlemen, all in mourning habits. He was received with every honour by King Charles and the whole Court, and, in a few days after his arrival, our marriage was solemnised with all possible magnificence; the King of Navarre and his retinue putting off their mourning and dressing themselves in the most costly manner. The whole Court, too, was richly attired; all which you can better conceive than I am able to express. For my own part, I was set out in a most royal manner; I wore a crown on my head with the 'coet', or regal close gown of ermine, and I blazed in diamonds. My blue-coloured robe had a train to it of four ells in length, which was supported by three princesses. A platform had been raised, some height from the ground, which led from the Bishop's palace to the Church of Notre-Dame. It was hung with cloth of gold; and below it stood the people in throngs to view the procession, stifling with heat. We were received at the church door by the Cardinal de Bourbon, who officiated for that day, and pronounced the nuptial benediction. After this we proceeded on the same platform to the tribune which separates the nave from the choir, where was a double staircase, one leading into the choir, the other through the nave to the church door. The King of Navarre passed by the latter and went out of church.

But fortune, which is ever changing, did not fail soon to disturb the felicity of this union. This was occasioned by the wound received by the Admiral, which had wrought the Huguenots up to a degree of desperation. The Queen my mother was reproached on that account in such terms by the elder Pardaillan and some other principal Huguenots, that she began to apprehend some evil design. M. de Guise and my brother the King of Poland, since Henri III. of France, gave it as their advice to be beforehand with the Huguenots. King Charles was of a contrary opinion. He had a great esteem for M. de La Rochefoucauld, Teligny, La Noue, and some other leading men of the same religion; and, as I have since heard him say, it was with the greatest difficulty he could be prevailed upon to give his consent, and not before he had been made to understand that his own life aid the safety of his kingdom depended upon it.

The King having learned that Maurevel had made an attempt upon the Admiral's life, by firing a pistol at him through a window,--in which attempt he failed, having wounded the Admiral only in the shoulder,--and supposing that Maurevel had done this at the instance of M. de Guise, to revenge the death of his father, whom the Admiral had caused to be killed in the same manner by Poltrot, he was so much incensed against M. de Guise that he declared with an oath that he would make an example of him; and, indeed, the King would have put M. de Guise under an arrest, if he had not kept out of his sight the whole day. The Queen my mother used every argument to convince King Charles that what had been done was for the good of the State; and this because, as I observed before, the King had so great a regard for the Admiral, La Noue, and Teligny, on account of their bravery, being himself a prince of a gallant and noble spirit, and esteeming others in whom he found a similar disposition. Moreover, these designing men had insinuated themselves into the King's favour by proposing an expedition to Flanders, with a view of extending his dominions and aggrandising his power, knew would secure to themselves an influence over his royal and generous mind.

Upon this occasion, the Queen my mother represented to the King that the attempt of M. de Guise upon the Admiral's life was excusable in a son who, being denied justice, had no other means of avenging his father's death. Moreover, the Admiral, she said, had deprived her by assassination, during his minority and her regency, of a faithful servant in the person of Charri, commander of the King's body-guard, which rendered him deserving of the like treatment.

Notwithstanding that the Queen my mother spoke thus to the King, discovering by her expressions and in her looks all the grief which she inwardly felt on the recollection of the loss of persons who had been useful to her; yet, so much was King Charles inclined to save those who, as he thought, would one day be serviceable to him, that he still persisted in his determination to punish M. de Guise, for whom he ordered strict search to be made.

At length Pardaillan, disclosing by his menaces, during the supper of the Queen my mother, the evil intentions of the Huguenots, she plainly perceived that things were brought to so near a crisis, that, unless steps were taken that very night to prevent it, the King and herself were in danger of being assassinated. She, therefore, came to the resolution of declaring to King Charles his real situation. For this purpose she thought of the Marechal de Rais as the most proper person to break the matter to the King, the Marshal being greatly in his favour and confidence.

Accordingly, the Marshal went to the King in his closet, between the hours of nine and ten, and told him he was come as a faithful servant to discharge his duty, and lay before him the danger in which he stood, if he persisted in his resolution of punishing M. de Guise, as he ought now to be informed that the attempt made upon the Admiral's life was not set on foot by him alone, but that his (the King's) brother the King of Poland, and the Queen his mother, had their shares in it; that he must be sensible how much the Queen lamented Charri's assassination, for which she had great reason, having very few servants about her upon whom she could rely, and as it happened during the King's minority,--at the time, moreover, when France was divided between the Catholics and the Huguenots, M. de Guise being at the head of the former, and the Prince de Conde of the latter, both alike striving to deprive him of his crown; that through Providence, both his crown and kingdom had been preserved by the prudence and good conduct of the Queen Regent, who in this extremity found herself powerfully aided by the said Charri, for which reason she had vowed to avenge his death; that, as to the Admiral, he must be ever considered as dangerous to the State, and whatever show he might make of affection for his Majesty's person, and zeal for his service in Flanders, they must be considered as mere pretences, which he used to cover his real design of reducing the kingdom to a state of confusion.

The Marshal concluded with observing that the original intention had been to make away with the Admiral only, as the most obnoxious man in the kingdom; but

Maurevel having been so unfortunate as to fail in his attempt, and the Huguenots becoming desperate enough to resolve to take up arms, with design to attack, not only M. de Guise, but the Queen his mother, and his brother the King of Poland, supposing them, as well as his Majesty, to have commanded Maurevel to make his attempt, he saw nothing but cause of alarm for his Majesty's safety,--as well on the part of the Catholics, if he persisted in his resolution to punish M. de Guise, as of the Huguenots, for the reasons which he had just laid before him.

LETTER V.

The Massacre of St. Bartholomew's Day.

King Charles, a prince of great prudence, always paying a particular deference to his mother, and being much attached to the Catholic religion, now convinced of the intentions of the Huguenots, adopted a sudden resolution of following his mother's counsel, and putting himself under the safeguard of the Catholics. It was not, however, without extreme regret that he found he had it not in his power to save Teligny, La Noue, and M. de La Rochefoucauld.

He went to the apartments of the Queen his mother, and sending for M. de Guise and all the Princes and Catholic officers, the "Massacre of St. Bartholomew" was that night resolved upon.

Immediately every hand was at work; chains were drawn across the streets, the alarm-bells were sounded, and every man repaired to his post, according to the orders he had received, whether it was to attack the Admiral's quarters, or those of the other Huguenots. M. de Guise hastened to the Admiral's, and Besme, a gentleman in the service of the former, a German by birth, forced into his chamber, and having slain him with a dagger, threw his body out of a window to his master.

I was perfectly ignorant of what was going forward. I observed every one to be in motion: the Huguenots, driven to despair by the attack upon the Admiral's life, and the Guises, fearing they should not have justice done them, whispering all they met in the ear.

The Huguenots were suspicious of me because I was a Catholic, and the Catholics because I was married to the King of Navarre, who was a Huguenot. This being the case, no one spoke a syllable of the matter to me.

At night, when I went into the bedchamber of the Queen my mother, I placed myself on a coffer, next my sister Lorraine, who, I could not but remark, appeared greatly cast down. The Queen my mother was in conversation with some one, but, as soon as she espied me, she bade me go to bed. As I was taking leave, my sister seized me by the hand and stopped me, at the same time shedding a flood of tears: "For the love of God," cried she, "do not stir out of this chamber!" I was greatly alarmed at this exclamation; perceiving which, the Queen my mother called my sister to her, and chid her very severely. My sister replied it was sending me away to be sacrificed; for, if any discovery should be made, I should be the first victim of their revenge. The Queen my mother made answer that, if it pleased God, I should receive no hurt, but it was necessary I should go, to prevent the suspicion that might arise from my staying.

I perceived there was something on foot which I was not to know, but what it was I could not make out from anything they said.

The Queen again bade me go to bed in a peremptory tone. My sister wished me a good night, her tears flowing apace, but she did not dare to say a word more; and I left the bedchamber more dead than alive.

As soon as I reached my own closet, I threw myself upon my knees and prayed to God to take me into his protection and save me; but from whom or what, I was ignorant. Hereupon the King my husband, who was already in bed, sent for me. I went to him, and found the bed surrounded by thirty or forty Huguenots, who were entirely unknown to me; for I had been then but a very short time married. Their whole discourse, during the night, was upon what had happened to the Admiral, and they all came to a resolution of the next day demanding justice of the King against M. de Guise; and, if it was refused, to take it themselves.

For my part, I was unable to sleep a wink the whole night, for thinking of my sister's tears and distress, which had greatly alarmed me, although I had not the least knowledge of the real cause. As soon as day broke, the King my husband said he would rise and play at tennis until King Charles was risen, when he would go to him immediately and demand justice. He left the bedchamber, and all his gentlemen followed.

As soon as I beheld it was broad day, I apprehended all the danger my sister had spoken of was over; and being inclined to sleep, I bade my nurse make the door fast, and I applied myself to take some repose. In about an hour I was awakened by a violent noise at the door, made with both hands and feet, and a voice calling out, "Navarre! Navarre!" My nurse, supposing the King my husband to be at the door, hastened to open it, when a gentleman, named M. de Teian, ran in, and threw himself immediately upon my bed. He had received a wound in his arm from a sword, and another by a pike, and was then pursued by four archers, who followed him into the bedchamber. Perceiving these last, I jumped out of bed, and the poor gentleman after me, holding me fast by the waist. I did not then know him; neither was I sure that he came to do me no harm, or whether the archers were in pursuit of him or me. In this situation I screamed aloud, and he cried out likewise, for our fright was mutual. At length, by God's providence, M. de Nangay, captain of the guard, came into the bed-chamber, and, seeing me thus surrounded, though he could not help pitying me, he was scarcely able to refrain from laughter. However, he reprimanded the archers very severely for their indiscretion, and drove them out of the chamber. At my request he granted the poor gentleman his life, and I had him put to bed in my closet, caused his wounds to be dressed, and did not suffer him to quit my apartment until he was perfectly cured. I changed my shift, because it was stained with the blood of this man, and, whilst I was doing so, De Nangay gave me an account of the transactions of the foregoing night, assuring me that the King my husband was safe, and actually at that moment in the King's bedchamber. He made me muffle myself up in a cloak, and conducted me to the apartment of my sister, Madame de Lorraine, whither I arrived more than half dead. As we passed through the antechamber, all the doors of which were wide open, a gentleman of the name of Bourse, pursued by archers, was run through the body with a pike, and fell dead at my feet. As if I had been killed by the same stroke, I fell, and was caught by M. de Nangay before I reached the ground. As soon as I recovered from this fainting-fit, I went into my sister's bedchamber, and was immediately followed by M. de Mioflano, first gentleman to the King my husband, and Armagnac, his first valet de chambre, who both came to beg me to save their lives. I went and threw myself on my knees before the King and the Queen my mother, and obtained the lives of both of them.

  Five or six days afterwards, those who were engaged in this plot, considering that it was incomplete whilst the King my husband and the Prince de Conde remained alive, as their design was not only to dispose of the Huguenots, but of the Princes of the blood likewise; and knowing that no attempt could be made on my husband whilst I continued to be his wife, devised a scheme which they suggested to the Queen my mother for divorcing me from him. Accordingly, one holiday, when I waited upon her to chapel, she charged me to declare to her, upon my oath, whether I believed my husband to be like other men. "Because," said she, "if he is not, I can easily procure you a divorce from him." I begged her to believe that I was not sufficiently competent to answer such a question, and could only reply, as the Roman lady did to her husband, when he chid her for not informing him of his stinking breath, that, never having approached any other man near enough to know a difference, she thought all men had been alike in that respect. "But," said I, "Madame, since you have put the question to me, I can only declare I am content to remain as I am;" and this I said because I suspected the design of separating me from my husband was in order to work some mischief against him.

LETTER VI.

Henri, Duc d'Anjou, Elected King of Poland, Leaves France.--Huguenot Plots to Withdraw the Duc d'Alencon and the King of Navarre from Court.--Discovered and Defeated by Marguerite's Vigilance.--She Draws Up an Eloquent Defence, Which Her Husband Delivers before a Committee from the Court of Parliament.--Alencon and Her Husband, under a Close Arrest, Regain Their Liberty by the Death of Charles IX.

We accompanied the King of Poland as far as Beaumont. For some months before he quitted France, he had used every endeavour to efface from my mind the ill offices he had so ungratefully done me. He solicited to obtain the same place in my esteem which he held during our infancy; and, on taking leave of me, made me confirm it by oaths and promises. His departure from France, and King Charles's sickness, which happened just about the same time, excited the spirit of the two factions into which the kingdom was divided, to form a variety of plots. The Huguenots, on the death of the Admiral, had obtained from the King my husband, and my brother Alencon, a written obligation to avenge it. Before St. Bartholomew's Day, they had gained my brother over to their party, by the hope of securing Flanders for him. They now persuaded my husband and him to leave the King and Queen on their return, and pass into Champagne, there to join some troops which were in waiting to receive them.

M. de Miossans, a Catholic gentleman, having received an intimation of this design, considered it so prejudicial to the interests of the King his master, that he communicated it to me with the intention of frustrating a plot of so much danger to themselves, and to the State. I went immediately to the King and the Queen my mother, and informed them that. I had a matter of the utmost importance to lay before them; but that I could not declare it unless they would be pleased to promise me that no harm should ensue from it to such as I should name to them, and that they would put a stop to what was going forward without publishing their knowledge of it. Having obtained my request, I told them that my brother Alencon and the King my husband had an intention, on the very next day, of joining some Huguenot troops, which expected them, in order to fulfil the engagement they had made upon the Admiral's death; and for this their intention, I begged they might be excused, and that they might be prevented from going away without any discovery being made that their designs had been found out. All this was granted me, and measures were so prudently taken to stay them, that they had not the least suspicion that their intended evasion was known. Soon after, we arrived at St. Germain, where we stayed some time, on account of the King's indisposition. All this while my brother Alencon used every means he could devise to ingratiate himself with me, until at last I promised him my friendship, as I had before done to my brother the King of Poland. As he had been brought up at a distance from Court, we had hitherto known very little of each other, and kept ourselves at a distance. Now that he had made the first advances, in so respectful and affectionate a manner, I resolved to receive him into a firm friendship, and to interest myself in whatever concerned him, without prejudice, however, to the interests of my good brother King Charles, whom I loved more than any one besides, and who continued to entertain a great regard for me, of which he gave me proofs as long as he lived.

Meanwhile King Charles was daily growing worse, and the Huguenots constantly forming new plots. They were very desirous to get my brother the Duc d'Alencon and the King my husband away from Court. I got intelligence, from time to time, of their designs; and, providentially, the Queen my mother defeated their intentions when a day had been fixed on for the arrival of the Huguenot troops at St. Germain.

To avoid this visit, we set off the night before for Paris, two hours after midnight, putting King Charles in a litter, and the Queen my mother taking my brother and the King my husband with her in her own carriage.

They did not experience on this occasion such mild treatment as they had hitherto done, for the King going to the Wood of Vincennes, they were not permitted to set foot out of the palace. This misunderstanding was so far from being mitigated by time, that the mistrust and discontent were continually increasing, owing to the insinuations and bad advice offered to the King by those who wished the ruin and downfall of our house. To such a height had these jealousies risen that the Marechaux de Montmorency and de Cosse were put under a close arrest, and La Mole and the Comte de Donas executed. Matters were now arrived at such a pitch that commissioners were appointed from the Court of Parliament to hear and determine upon the case of my brother and the King my husband.

My husband, having no counsellor to assist him, desired me to draw up his defence in such a manner that he might not implicate any person, and, at the same time, clear my brother and himself from any criminality of conduct. With God's help I accomplished this task to his great satisfaction, and to the surprise of the commissioners, who did not expect to find them so well prepared to justify themselves.

As it was apprehended, after the death of La Mole and the Comte de Donas, that their lives were likewise in danger, I had resolved to save them at the hazard of my own ruin with the King, whose favour I entirely enjoyed at that time. I was suffered to pass to and from them in my coach, with my women, who were not even required by the guard to unmask, nor was my coach ever searched. This being the case, I had intended to convey away one of them disguised in a female habit. But the difficulty lay in settling betwixt themselves which should remain behind in prison, they being closely watched by their guards, and the escape of one bringing the other's life into hazard. Thus they could never agree upon the point, each of them wishing to be the person I should deliver from confinement.

But Providence put a period to their imprisonment by a means which proved very unfortunate for me. This was no other than the death of King Charles, who was the only stay and support of my life,--a brother from whose hands I never received anything but good; who, during the persecution I underwent at Angers, through my brother Anjou, assisted me with all his advice and credit. In a word, when I lost King Charles, I lost everything.

LETTER VII.

Accession of Henri III.--A Journey to Lyons.--Marguerite's Faith in Supernatural Intelligence.

After this fatal event, which was as unfortunate for France as for me, we went to Lyons to give the meeting to the King of Poland, now Henri III. of France. The new King was as much governed by Le Guast as ever, and had left this intriguing, mischievous man behind in France to keep his party together. Through this man's insinuations he had conceived the most confirmed jealousy of my brother Alencon. He suspected that I was the bond that connected the King my husband and my brother, and that, to dissolve their union, it would be necessary to create a coolness between me and my husband, and to work up a quarrel of rivalship betwixt them both by means of Madame de Sauves, whom they both visited. This abominable plot, which proved the source of so much disquietude and unhappiness, as well to my brother as myself, was as artfully conducted as it was wickedly designed.

Many have held that God has great personages more immediately under his protection, and that minds of superior excellence have bestowed on them a good genius, or secret intelligencer, to apprise them of good, or warn them against evil. Of this number I might reckon the Queen my mother, who has had frequent intimations of the kind; particularly the very night before the tournament which proved so fatal to the King my father, she dreamed that she saw him wounded in the eye, as it really happened; upon which she awoke, and begged him not to run a course that day, but content himself with looking on. Fate prevented the nation from enjoying so much happiness as it would have done had he followed her advice. Whenever she lost a child, she beheld a bright flame shining before her, and would immediately cry out, "God save my children!" well knowing it was the harbinger of the death of some one of them, which melancholy news was sure to be confirmed very shortly after. During her very dangerous illness at Metz, where she caught a pestilential fever, either from the coal fires, or by visiting some of the nunneries which had been infected, and from which she was restored to health and to the kingdom through the great skill and experience of that modern Asculapius, M. de Castilian, her physician--I say, during that illness, her bed being surrounded by my brother King Charles, my brother and sister Lorraine, several members of the Council, besides many ladies and princesses, not choosing to quit her, though without hopes of her life, she was heard to cry out, as if she saw the battle of Jarnac: "There! see how they flee! My son, follow them to victory! Ah, my son falls! O my God, save him! See there! the Prince de Conde is dead!" All who were present looked upon these words as proceeding from her delirium, as she knew that my brother Anjou was on the point of giving battle, and thought no more of it. On the night following, M. de Losses brought the news of the battle; and, it being supposed that she would be pleased to hear of it, she was awakened, at which she appeared to be angry, saying: "Did I not know it yesterday?" It was then that those about her recollected what I have now related, and concluded that it was no delirium, but one of those revelations made by God to great and illustrious persons. Ancient history furnishes many examples of the like kind amongst the pagans, as the apparition of Brutus and many others, which I shall not mention, it not being my intention to illustrate these Memoirs with such narratives, but only to relate the truth, and that with as much expedition as I am able, that you may be the sooner in possession of my story.

I am far from supposing that I am worthy of these divine admonitions; nevertheless, I should accuse myself of ingratitude towards my God for the benefits I have received, which I esteem myself obliged to acknowledge whilst I live; and I further believe myself bound to bear testimony of his goodness and power, and the mercies he hath shown me, so that I can declare no extraordinary accident ever befell me, whether fortunate or otherwise, but I received some warning of it, either by dream or in some other way, so that I may say with the poet

"De mon bien, on mon mal, Mon esprit m'est oracle."

(Whate'er of good or ill befell, My mind was oracle to tell.)

And of this I had a convincing proof on the arrival of the King of Poland, when the Queen my mother went to meet him. Amidst the embraces and compliments of welcome in that warm season, crowded as we were together and stifling with heat, I found a universal shivering come over me, which was plainly perceived by those near me. It was with difficulty I could conceal what I felt when the King, having saluted the Queen my mother, came forward to salute me. This secret intimation of what was to happen thereafter made a strong impression on my mind at the moment, and I thought of it shortly after, when I discovered that the King had conceived a hatred of me through the malicious suggestions of Le Guast, who had made him believe, since the King's death, that I espoused my brother Alencon's party during his absence, and cemented a friendship betwixt the King my husband and him.

LETTER VIII.

What Happened at Lyons.

An opportunity was diligently sought by my enemies to effect their design of bringing about a misunderstanding betwixt my brother Alencon, the King my husband, and me, by creating a jealousy of me in my husband, and in my brother and husband, on account of their mutual love for Madame de Sauves.

One afternoon, the Queen my mother having retired to her closet to finish some despatches which were likely to detain her there for some time, Madame de Nevers, your kinswoman, Madame de Rais, another of your relations, Bourdeille, and Surgeres asked me whether I would not wish to see a little of the city. Whereupon Mademoiselle de Montigny, the niece of Madame Usez, observing to us that the Abbey of St. Pierre was a beautiful convent, we all resolved to visit it. She then begged to go with us, as she said she had an aunt in that convent, and as it was not easy to gain admission into it, except in the company of persons of distinction. Accordingly, she went with us; and there being six of us, the carriage was crowded. Over and above those I have mentioned, there was Madame de Curton, the lady of my bedchamber, who always attended me. Liancourt, first esquire to the King, and Camille placed themselves on the steps of Torigni's carriage, supporting themselves as well as they were able, making themselves merry on the occasion, and saying they would go and see the handsome nuns, too. I look upon it as ordered by Divine Providence that I should have Mademoiselle de Montigny with me, who was not well acquainted with any lady of the company, and that the two gentlemen just mentioned, who were in the confidence of King Henri, should likewise be of the party, as they were able to clear me of the calumny intended to be fixed upon me.

Whilst we were viewing the convent, my carriage waited for us in the square. In the square many gentlemen belonging to the Court had their lodgings. My carriage was easily to be distinguished, as it was gilt and lined with yellow velvet trimmed with silver. We had not come out of the convent when the King passed through the square on his way to see Quelus, who was then sick. He had with him the King my husband, D'O------, and the fat fellow Ruff.

The King, observing no one in my carriage, turned to my husband and said: "There is your wife's coach, and that is the house where Bide lodges. Bide is sick, and I will engage my word she is gone upon a visit to him. Go," said he to Ruff, "and see whether she is not there." In saying this, the King addressed himself to a proper tool for his malicious purpose, for this fellow Ruffs was entirely devoted to Le Guast. I need not tell you he did not find me there; however, knowing the King's intention, he, to favour it, said loud enough for the King my husband to hear him: "The birds have been there, but they are now flown." This furnished sufficient matter for conversation until they reached home.

Upon this occasion, the King my husband displayed all the good sense and generosity of temper for which he is remarkable. He saw through the design, and he despised the maliciousness of it. The King my brother was anxious to see the Queen my mother before me, to whom he imparted the pretended discovery, and she, whether to please a son on whom she doted, or whether she really gave credit to the story, had related it to some ladies with much seeming anger.

Soon afterwards I returned with the ladies who had accompanied me to St. Pierre's, entirely ignorant of what had happened. I found the King my husband in our apartments, who began to laugh on seeing me, and said: "Go immediately to the Queen your mother, but I promise you you will not return very well pleased." I asked him the reason, and what had happened. He answered: "I shall tell you nothing; but be assured of this, that I do not give the least credit to the story, which I plainly perceive to be fabricated in order to stir up a difference betwixt us two, and break off the friendly intercourse between your brother and me."

Finding I could get no further information on the subject from him, I went to the apartment of the Queen my mother. I met M. de Guise in the antechamber, who was not displeased at the prospect of a dissension in our family, hoping that he might make some advantage of it. He addressed me in these words: "I waited here expecting to see you, in order to inform you that some ill office has been done you with the Queen." He then told me the story he had learned of D'O------, who, being intimate with your kinswoman, had informed M. de Guise of it, that he might apprise us.

I went into the Queen's bedchamber, but did not find my mother there. However, I saw Madame de Nemours, the rest of the princesses, and other ladies, who all exclaimed on seeing me: "Good God! the Queen your mother is in such a rage; we would advise you, for the present, to keep out of her sight."

"Yes," said I, "so I would, had I been guilty of what the King has reported; but I assure you all I am entirely innocent, and must therefore speak with her and clear myself."

I then went into her closet, which was separated from the bedchamber by a slight partition only, so that our whole conversation could be distinctly heard. She no sooner set eyes upon me than she flew into a great passion, and said everything that the fury of her resentment suggested. I related to her the whole truth, and begged to refer her to the company which attended me, to the number of ten or twelve persons, desiring her not to rely on the testimony of those more immediately about me, but examine Mademoiselle Montigny, who did not belong to me, and Liancourt and Camille, who were the King's servants.

She would not hear a word I had to offer, but continued to rate me in a furious manner; whether it was through fear, or affection for her son, or whether she believed the story in earnest, I know not. When I observed to her that I understood the King had done me this ill office in her opinion, her anger was redoubled, and she endeavoured to make me believe that she had been informed of the circumstance by one of her own valets de chambre, who had himself seen me at the place. Perceiving that I gave no credit to this account of the matter, she became more and more incensed against me.

All that was said was perfectly heard by those in the next room. At length I left her closet, much chagrined; and returning to my own apartments, I found the King my husband there, who said to me:

"Well, was it not as I told you?"

He, seeing me under great concern, desired me not to grieve about it, adding that "Liancourt and Camille would attend the King that night in his bedchamber, and relate the affair as it really was; and to-morrow," continued he, "the Queen your mother will receive you in a very different manner."

"But, monsieur," I replied, "I have received too gross an affront in public to forgive those who were the occasion of it; but that is nothing when compared with the malicious intention of causing so heavy a misfortune to befall me as to create a variance betwixt you and me."

"But," said he, "God be thanked, they have failed in it."

"For that," answered I, "I am the more beholden to God and your amiable disposition. However," continued I, "we may derive this good from it, that it ought to be a warning to us to put ourselves upon our guard against the King's stratagems to bring about a disunion betwixt you and my brother, by causing a rupture betwixt you and me."

Whilst I was saying this, my brother entered the apartment, and I made them renew their protestations of friendship. But what oaths or promises can prevail against love! This will appear more fully in the sequel of my story.

An Italian banker, who had concerns with my brother, came to him the next morning, and invited him, the King my husband, myself, the princesses, and other ladies, to partake of an entertainment in a garden belonging to him. Having made it a constant rule, before and after I married, as long as I remained in the Court of the Queen my mother, to go to no place without her permission, I waited on her, at her return from mass, and asked leave to be present at this banquet. She refused to give any leave, and said she did not care where I went. I leave you to judge, who know my temper, whether I was not greatly mortified at this rebuff.

Whilst we were enjoying this entertainment, the King, having spoken with Liancourt, Camille, and Mademoiselle Montigny, was apprised of the mistake which the malice or misapprehension of Ruff had led him into. Accordingly, he went to the Queen my mother and related the whole truth, entreating her to remove any ill impressions that might remain with me, as he perceived that I was not deficient in point of understanding, and feared that I might be induced to engage in some plan of revenge.

When I returned from the banquet before mentioned, I found that what the King my husband had foretold was come to pass; for the Queen my mother sent for me into her back closet, which was adjoining the King's, and told me that she was now acquainted with the truth, and found I had not deceived her with a false story. She had discovered, she said, that there was not the least foundation for the report her valet de chambre had made, and should dismiss him from her service as a bad man. As she perceived by my looks that I saw through this disguise, she said everything she could think of to persuade me to a belief that the King had not mentioned it to her. She continued her arguments, and I still appeared incredulous. At length the King entered the closet, and made many apologies, declaring he had been imposed on, and assuring me of his most cordial friendship and esteem; and thus matters were set to rights again.

LETTER IX.

Fresh Intrigues.--Marriage of Henri III.--Bussi Arrives at Court and Narrowly Escapes Assassination.

After staying some time at Lyons, we went to Avignon. Le Guast, not daring to hazard any fresh imposture, and finding that my conduct afforded no ground for jealousy on the part of my husband, plainly perceived that he could not, by that means, bring about a misunderstanding betwixt my brother and the King my husband. He therefore resolved to try what he could effect through Madame de Sauves. In order to do this, he obtained such an influence over her that she acted entirely as he directed; insomuch that, by his artful instructions, the passion which these young men had conceived, hitherto wavering and cold, as is generally the case at their time of life, became of a sudden so violent that ambition and every obligation of duty were at once absorbed by their attentions to this woman.

This occasioned such a jealousy betwixt them that, though her favours were divided with M. de Guise, Le Guast, De Souvray, and others, any one of whom she preferred to the brothers-in-law, such was the infatuation of these last, that each considered the other as his only rival.

To carry on De Guast's sinister designs, this woman persuaded the King my husband that I was jealous of her, and on that account it was that I joined with my brother. As we are ready to give ear and credit to those we love, he believed all she said. From this time he became distant and reserved towards me, shunning my presence as much as possible; whereas, before, he was open and communicative to me as to a sister, well knowing that I yielded to his pleasure in all things, and was far from harbouring jealousy of any kind.

What I had dreaded, I now perceived had come to pass. This was the loss of his favour and good opinion; to preserve which I had studied to gain his confidence by a ready compliance with his wishes, well knowing that mistrust is the sure forerunner of hatred.

I now turned my mind to an endeavour to wean my brother's affection from Madame de Sauves, in order to counterplot Le Guast in his design to bring about a division, and thereby to effect our ruin. I used every means with my brother to divert his passion; but the fascination was too strong, and my pains proved ineffectual. In anything else, my brother would have suffered himself to be ruled by me; but the charms of this Circe, aided by that sorcerer, Le Guast, were too powerful to be dissolved by my advice. So far was he from profiting by my counsel that he was weak enough to communicate it to her. So blind are lovers!

Her vengeance was excited by this communication, and she now entered more fully into the designs of Le Guast. In consequence, she used all her art to, make the King my husband conceive an aversion for me; insomuch that he scarcely ever spoke with me. He left her late at night, and, to prevent our meeting in the morning, she directed him to come to her at the Queen's levee, which she duly attended; after which he passed the rest of the day with her. My brother likewise followed her with the greatest assiduity, and she had the artifice to make each of them think that he alone had any place in her esteem. Thus was a jealousy kept up betwixt them, and, in consequence, disunion and mutual ruin.

We made a considerable stay at Avignon, whence we proceeded through Burgundy and Champagne to Rheims, where the King's marriage was celebrated. From Rheims we came to Paris, things going on in their usual train, and Le Guast prosecuting his designs, with all the success he could wish. At Paris my brother was joined by Bussi, whom he received with all the favour which his bravery merited. He was inseparable from my brother, in consequence of which I frequently saw him, for my brother and I were always together, his household being equally at my devotion as if it were my own. Your aunt, remarking this harmony betwixt us, has often told me that it called to her recollection the times of my uncle, M. d'Orleans, and my aunt, Madame de Savoie.

Le Guast thought this a favourable circumstance to complete his design. Accordingly, he suggested to Madame de Sauves to make my husband believe that it was on account of Bussi that I frequented my brother's apartments so constantly.

The King my husband, being fully informed of all my proceedings from persons in his service who attended me everywhere, could not be induced to lend an ear to this story. Le Guast, finding himself foiled in this quarter, applied to the King, who was well inclined to listen to the tale, on account of his dislike to my brother and me, whose friendship for each other was unpleasing to him.

Besides this, he was incensed against Bussi, who, being formerly attached to him, had now devoted himself wholly to my brother,--an acquisition which, on account of the celebrity of Bussi's fame for parts and valour, redounded greatly to my brother's honour, whilst it increased the malice and envy of his enemies.

The King, thus worked upon by Le Guast, mentioned it to the Queen my mother, thinking it would have the same effect on her as the tale which was trumped up at Lyons. But she, seeing through the whole design, showed him the improbability of the story, adding that he must have some wicked people about him, who could put such notions in his head, observing that I was very unfortunate to have fallen upon such evil times. "In my younger days," said she, "we were allowed to converse freely with all the gentlemen who belonged to the King our father, the Dauphin, and M. d'Orleans, your uncles. It was common for them to assemble in the bedchamber of Madame Marguerite, your aunt, as well as in mine, and nothing was thought of it. Neither ought it to appear strange that Bussi sees my daughter in the presence of her husband's servants. They are not shut up together. Bussi is a person of quality, and holds the first place in your brother's family. What grounds are there for such a calumny? At Lyons you caused me to offer her an affront, which I fear she will never forget."

The King was astonished to hear his mother talk in this manner, and interrupted her with saying:

"Madame, I only relate what I have heard."

"But who is it," answered she, "that tells you all this? I fear no one that intends you any good, but rather one that wishes to create divisions amongst you all."

As soon as the King had left her she told me all that had passed, and said: "You are unfortunate to live in these times." Then calling your aunt, Madame de Dampierre, they entered into a discourse concerning the pleasures and innocent freedoms of the times they had seen, when scandal and malevolence were unknown at

Court.

Le Guast, finding this plot miscarry, was not long in contriving another. He addressed himself for this purpose to certain gentlemen who attended the King my husband. These had been formerly the friends of Bussi, but, envying the glory he had obtained, were now become his enemies. Under the mask of zeal for their master, they disguised the envy, which they harboured in their breasts. They entered into a design of assassinating Bussi as he left my brother to go to his own lodgings, which was generally at a late hour. They knew that he was always accompanied home by fifteen or sixteen gentlemen, belonging to my brother, and that, notwithstanding he wore no sword, having been lately wounded in the right arm, his presence was sufficient to inspire the rest with courage.

In order, therefore, to make sure work, they resolved on attacking him with two or three hundred men, thinking that night would throw a veil over the disgrace of such an assassination.

Le Guast, who commanded a regiment of guards, furnished the requisite number of men, whom he disposed in five or six divisions, in the street through which he was to pass. Their orders were to put out the torches and flambeaux, and then to fire their pieces, after which they were to charge his company, observing particularly to attack one who had his right arm slung in a scarf.

Fortunately they escaped the intended massacre, and, fighting their way through, reached Bussi's lodgings, one gentleman only being killed, who was particularly attached to M. de Bussi, and who was probably mistaken for him, as he had his arm likewise slung in a scarf.

An Italian gentleman, who belonged to my brother, left them at the beginning of the attack, and came running back to the Louvre. As soon as he reached my brother's chamber door, he cried out aloud:

"Busai is assassinated!" My brother was going out, but I, hearing the cry of assassination, left my chamber, by good fortune not being undressed, and stopped my brother. I then sent for the Queen my mother to come with all haste in order to prevent him from going out, as he was resolved to do, regardless of what might happen. It was with difficulty we could stay him, though the Queen my mother represented the hazard he ran from the darkness of the night, and his ignorance of the nature of the attack, which might have been purposely designed by Le Guast to take away his life. Her entreaties and persuasions would have been of little avail if she had not used her authority to order all the doors to be barred, and taken the resolution of remaining where she was until she had learned what had really happened.

Bussi, whom God had thus miraculously preserved, with that presence of mind which he was so remarkable for in time of battle and the most imminent danger, considering within himself when he reached home the anxiety of his master's mind should he have received any false report, and fearing he might expose himself to hazard upon the first alarm being given (which certainly would have been the case, if my mother had not interfered and prevented it), immediately despatched one of his people to let him know every circumstance.

The next day Busai showed himself at the Louvre without the least dread of enemies, as if what had happened had been merely the attack of a tournament. My brother exhibited much pleasure at the sight of Busai, but expressed great resentment at such a daring attempt to deprive him of so brave and valuable a servant, a man whom Le Guast durst not attack in any other way than by a base assassination.

LETTER X.

Bussi Is Sent from Court.--Marguerite's Husband Attacked with a Fit of Epilepsy.--Her Great Care of Him.--Torigni Dismissed from Marguerite's Service.--The King of Navarre and the Duc d'Alencon Secretly Leave the Court.

The Queen my mother, a woman endowed with the greatest prudence and foresight of any one I ever knew, apprehensive of evil consequences from this affair, and fearing a dissension betwixt her two sons, advised my brother to fall upon some pretence for sending Bussi away from Court. In this advice I joined her, and, through our united counsel and request, my brother was prevailed upon to give his consent. I had every reason to suppose that Le Guast would take advantage of the reencounter to foment the coolness which already existed betwixt my brother and the King my husband into an open rupture. Bussi, who implicitly followed my brother's directions in everything, departed with a company of the bravest noblemen that were about the latter's person.

Bussi was now removed from the machinations of Le Guast, who likewise failed in accomplishing a design he had long projected,--to disunite the King my husband and me.

One night my husband was attacked with a fit, and continued insensible for the space of an hour,--occasioned, I supposed, by his excesses with women, for I never knew anything of the kind to happen to him before. However, as it was my duty so to do, I attended him with so much care and assiduity that, when he recovered, he spoke of it to every one, declaring that, if I had not perceived his indisposition and called for the help of my women, he should not have survived the fit.

From this time he treated me with more kindness, and the cordiality betwixt my brother and him was again revived, as if I had been the point of union at which they were to meet, or the cement that joined them together.

Le Guast was now at his wit's end for some fresh contrivance to breed disunion in the Court.

He had lately persuaded the King to remove from about the person of the Queen-consort a princess of the greatest virtue and most amiable qualities, a female attendant of the name of Changi, for whom the Queen entertained a particular esteem, as having been brought up with her. Being successful in this measure, he now thought of making the King my husband send away Torigni, whom I greatly regarded.

The argument he used with the King was, that young princesses ought to have no favourites about them.

The King, yielding to this man's persuasions, spoke of it to my husband, who observed that it would be a matter that would greatly distress me; that if I had an esteem for Torigni it was not without cause, as she had been brought up with the Queen of Spain and me from our infancy; that, moreover, Torigni was a young lady of good understanding, and had been of great use to him during his confinement at Vincennes; that it would be the greatest ingratitude in him to overlook services of such a nature, and that he remembered well when his Majesty had expressed the same sentiments.

Thus did he defend himself against the performance of so ungrateful an action. However, the King listened only to the arguments of Le Guast, and told my husband that he should have no more love for him if he did not remove Torigni from about me the very next morning.

He was forced to comply, greatly contrary to his will, and, as he has since declared to me, with much regret. Joining entreaties to commands, he laid his injunctions on me accordingly.

How displeasing this separation was I plainly discovered by the many tears I shed on receiving his orders. It was in vain to represent to him the injury done to my character by the sudden removal of one who had been with me from my earliest years, and was so greatly, in my esteem and confidence; he could not give an ear to my reasons, being firmly bound by the promise he had made to the King.

Accordingly, Torigni left me that very day, and went to the house of a relation, M. Chastelas. I was so greatly offended with this fresh indignity, after so many of the kind formerly received, that I could not help yielding to resentment; and my grief and concern getting the upper hand of my prudence, I exhibited a great coolness and indifference towards my husband. Le Guast and Madame de Sauves were successful in creating a like indifference on his part, which, coinciding with mine, separated us altogether, and we neither spoke to each other nor slept in the same bed.

A few days after this, some faithful servants about the person of the King my husband remarked to him the plot which had been concerted with so much artifice to lead him to his ruin, by creating a division, first betwixt him and my brother, and next betwixt him and me, thereby separating him from those in whom only he could hope for his principal support. They observed to him that already matters were brought to such a pass that the King showed little regard for him, and even appeared to despise him.

They afterwards addressed themselves to my brother, whose situation was not in the least mended since the departure of Bussi, Le Guast causing fresh indignities to be offered him daily. They represented to him that the King my husband and he were both circumstanced alike, and equally in disgrace, as Le Guast had everything under his direction; so that both of them were under the necessity of soliciting, through him, any favours which they might want of the King, and which, when demanded, were constantly refused them with great contempt. Moreover, it was become dangerous to offer them service, as it was inevitable ruin for any one to do so.

"Since, then," said they, "your dissensions appear to be so likely to prove fatal to both, it would be advisable in you both to unite and come to a determination of leaving the Court; and, after collecting together your friends and servants, to require from the King an establishment suitable to your ranks." They observed to my brother that he had never yet been put in possession of his appanage, and received for his subsistence only some certain allowances, which were not regularly paid him, as they passed through the hands of Le Guast, and were at his disposal, to be discharged or kept back, as he judged proper. They concluded with observing that, with regard to the King my husband, the government of Guyenne was taken out of his hands; neither was he permitted to visit that or any other of his dominions.

It was hereupon resolved to pursue the counsel now given, and that the King my husband and my brother should immediately withdraw themselves from Court. My brother made me acquainted with this resolution, observing to me, as my husband and he were now friends again, that I ought to forget all that had passed; that my husband had declared to him that he was sorry things had so happened, that we had been outwitted by our enemies, but that he was resolved, from henceforward, to show me every attention and give me every proof of his love and esteem, and he concluded with begging me to make my husband every show of affection, and to be watchful for their interest during their absence.

It was concerted betwixt them that my brother should depart first, making off in a carriage in the best manner he could; that, in a few days afterwards, the King my husband should follow, under pretence of going on a hunting party. They both expressed their concern that they could not take me with them, assuring me that I had no occasion to have any apprehensions, as it would soon appear that they had no design to disturb the peace of the kingdom, but merely to ensure the safety of their own persons, and to settle their establishments. In short, it might well be supposed that, in their present situation, they had danger to themselves from such reason to apprehend as had evil designs against their family.

Accordingly, as soon as it was dusk, and before the King's supper-time, my brother changed his cloak, and concealing the lower part of his face to his nose in it, left the palace, attended by a servant who was little known, and went on foot to the gate of St. Honore, where he found Simier waiting for him in a coach, borrowed of a lady for the purpose.

My brother threw himself into it, and went to a house about a quarter of a league out of Paris, where horses were stationed ready; and at the distance of about a league farther, he joined a party of two or three hundred horsemen of his servants, who were awaiting his coming. My brother was not missed till nine o'clock, when the King and the Queen my mother asked me the reason he did not come to sup with them as usual, and if I knew of his being indisposed. I told them I had not seen him since noon. Thereupon they sent to his apartments. Word was brought back that he was not there. Orders were then given to inquire at the apartments of the ladies whom he was accustomed to visit. He was nowhere to be found. There was now a general alarm. The King flew into a great passion, and began to threaten me. He then sent for all the Princes and the great officers of the Court; and giving orders for a pursuit to be made, and to bring him back, dead or alive, cried out:

"He is gone to make war against me; but I will show him what it is to contend with a king of my power."

Many of the Princes and officers of State remonstrated against these orders, which they observed ought to be well weighed. They said that, as their duty directed, they were willing to venture their lives in the King's service; but to act against his brother they were certain would not be pleasing to the King himself; that they were well convinced his brother would undertake nothing that should give his Majesty displeasure, or be productive of danger to the realm; that perhaps his leaving the Court was owing to some disgust, which it would be more advisable to send and inquire into. Others, on the contrary, were for putting the King's orders into execution; but, whatever expedition they could use, it was day before they set off; and as it was then too late to overtake my brother, they returned, being only equipped for the pursuit.

I was in tears the whole night of my brother's departure, and the next day was seized with a violent cold, which was succeeded by a fever that confined me to my bed.

Meanwhile my husband was preparing for his departure, which took up all the time he could spare from his visits to Madame de Sauves; so that he did not think of me. He returned as usual at two or three in the morning, and, as we had separate beds, I seldom heard him; and in the morning, before I was awake, he went to my mother's levee, where he met Madame de Sauves, as usual.

This being the case, he quite forgot his promise to my brother of speaking to me; and when he went, away, it was without taking leave of me.

The King did not show my husband more favour after my brother's evasion, but continued to behave with his former coolness. This the more confirmed him in the resolution of leaving the Court, so that in a few days, under the pretence of hunting, he went away.

LETTER XI.

Queen Marguerite under Arrest.--Attempt on Torigni's Life.--Her Fortunate Deliverance.

The King, supposing that I was a principal instrument in aiding the Princes in their desertion, was greatly incensed against me, and his rage became at length so violent that, had not the Queen my mother moderated it, I am inclined to think my life had been in danger. Giving way to her counsel, he became more calm, but insisted upon a guard being placed over me, that I might not follow the King my husband, neither have communication with any one, so as to give the Princes intelligence of what was going on at Court. The Queen my mother gave her consent to this measure, as being the least violent, and was well pleased to find his anger cooled in so great a degree. She, however, requested that she might be permitted to discourse with me, in order to reconcile me to a submission to treatment of so different a kind from what I had hitherto known. At the same time she advised the King to consider that these troubles might not be lasting; that everything in the world bore a double aspect; that what now appeared to him horrible and alarming, might, upon a second view, assume a more pleasing and tranquil look; that, as things changed, so should measures change with them; that there might come a time when he might have occasion for my services; that, as prudence counselled us not to repose too much confidence in our friends, lest they should one day become our enemies, so was it advisable to conduct ourselves in such a manner to our enemies as if we had hopes they should hereafter become our friends. By such prudent remonstrances did the Queen my mother restrain the King from proceeding to extremities with me, as he would otherwise possibly have done.

Le Guast now endeavoured to divert his fury to another object, in order to wound me in a most sensitive part. He prevailed on the King to adopt a design for seizing Torigni, at the house of her cousin Chastelas, and, under pretence of bringing her before the King, to drown her in a river which they were to cross. The party sent upon this errand was admitted by Chastelas, not suspecting any evil design, without the least difficulty, into his house. As soon as they had gained admission they proceeded to execute the cruel business they were sent upon, by fastening Torigni with cords and locking her up in a chamber, whilst their horses were baiting. Meantime, according to the French custom, they crammed themselves, like gluttons, with the best eatables the house afforded.

Chastelas, who was a man of discretion, was not displeased to gain time at the expense of some part of his substance, considering that the suspension of a sentence is a prolongation of life, and that during this respite the King's heart might relent, and he might countermand his former orders. With these considerations he was induced to submit, though it was in his power to have called for assistance to repel this violence. But God, who hath constantly regarded my afflictions and afforded me protection against the malicious designs of my enemies, was pleased to order poor Torigni to be delivered by means which I could never have devised had I been acquainted with the plot, of which I was totally ignorant. Several of the domestics, male as well as female, had left the house in a fright, fearing the insolence and rude treatment of this troop of soldiers, who behaved as riotously as if they were in a house given up to pillage. Some of these, at the distance of a quarter of a league from the house, by God's providence, fell in with Ferte and Avantigni, at the head of their troops, in number about two hundred horse, on their march to join my brother. Ferte, remarking a labourer, whom he knew to belong to Chastelas, apparently in great distress, inquired of him what was the matter, and whether he had been ill-used by any of the soldiery. The man related to him all he knew, and in what state he had left his master's house. Hereupon Ferte and Avantigni resolved, out of regard to me, to effect Torigni's deliverance, returning thanks to God for having afforded them so favourable an opportunity of testifying the respect they had always entertained towards me.

Accordingly, they proceeded to the house with all expedition, and arrived just at the moment these soldiers were setting Torigni on horseback, for the purpose of conveying her to the river wherein they had orders to plunge her. Galloping into the courtyard, sword in hand, they cried out: "Assassins, if you dare to offer that lady the least injury, you are dead men!" So saying, they attacked them and drove them to flight, leaving their prisoner behind, nearly as dead with joy as she was before with fear and apprehension. After returning thanks to God and her deliverers for so opportune and unexpected a rescue, she and her cousin Chastelas set off in a carriage, under the escort of their rescuers, and joined my brother, who, since he could not have me with him, was happy to have one so dear to me about him. She remained under my brother's protection as long as any danger was apprehended, and was treated with as much respect as if she had been with me.

Whilst the King was giving directions for this notable expedition, for the purpose of sacrificing Torigni to his vengeance, the Queen my mother, who had not received the least intimation of it, came to my apartment as I was dressing to go abroad, in order to observe how I should be received after what had passed at Court, having still some alarms on account of my husband and brother. I had hitherto confined myself to my chamber, not having perfectly recovered my health, and, in reality, being all the time as much indisposed in mind as in body.

My mother, perceiving my intention, addressed me in these words: "My child, you are giving yourself unnecessary trouble in dressing to go abroad. Do not be alarmed at what I am going to tell you. Your own good sense will dictate to you that you ought not to be surprised if the King resents the conduct of your brother and husband, and as he knows the love and friendship that exist between you three, should suppose that you were privy to their design of leaving the Court. He has, for this reason, resolved to detain you in it, as a hostage for them. He is sensible how much you are beloved by your husband, and thinks he can hold no pledge that is more dear to him. On this account it is that the King has ordered his guards to be placed, with directions not to suffer you to leave your apartments. He has done this with the advice of his counsellors, by whom it was suggested that, if you had your free liberty, you might be induced to advise your brother and husband of their deliberations. I beg you will not be offended with these measures, which, if it so please God, may not be of long continuance. I beg, moreover, you will not be displeased with me if I do not pay you frequent visits, as I should be unwilling to create any suspicions in the King's mind. However, you may rest assured that I shall prevent any further steps from being taken that may prove disagreeable to you, and that I shall use my utmost endeavours to bring about a reconciliation betwixt your brothers."

I represented to her, in reply, the great indignity that was offered to me by putting me under arrest; that it was true my brother had all along communicated to me the just cause he had to be dissatisfied, but that, with respect to the King my husband, from the time Torigni was taken from me we had not spoken to each other; neither had he visited me during my indisposition, nor did he even take leave of me when he left Court. "This," says she, "is nothing at all; it is merely a trifling difference betwixt man and wife, which a few sweet words, conveyed in a letter, will set to rights. When, by such means, he has regained your affections, he has only to write to you to come to him, and you will set off at the very first opportunity. Now, this is what the King my son wishes to prevent."

LETTER XII.

The Peace of Sens betwixt Henri III. and the Huguenots.

The Queen my mother left me, saying these words. For my part, I remained a close prisoner, without a visit from a single person, none of my most intimate friends daring to come near me, through the apprehension that such a step might prove injurious to their interests. Thus it is ever in Courts. Adversity is solitary, while prosperity dwells in a crowd; the object of persecution being sure to be shunned by his nearest friends and dearest connections. The brave Grillon was the only one who ventured to visit me, at the hazard of incurring disgrace. He came five or six times to see me, and my guards were so much astonished at his resolution, and awed by his presence, that not a single Cerberus of them all would venture to refuse him entrance to my apartments.

Meanwhile, the King my husband reached the States under his government. Being joined there by his friends and dependents, they all represented to him the indignity offered to me by his quitting the Court without taking leave of me. They observed to him that I was a princess of good understanding, and that it would be for his interest to regain my esteem; that, when matters were put on their former footing, he might derive to himself great advantage from my presence at Court. Now that he was at a distance from his Circe, Madame de Sauves, he could listen to good advice. Absence having abated the force of her charms, his eyes were opened; he discovered the plots and machinations of our enemies, and clearly perceived that a rupture could not but tend to the ruin of us both.

Accordingly, he wrote me a very affectionate letter, wherein he entreated me to forget all that had passed betwixt us, assuring me that from thenceforth he would ever love me, and would give me every demonstration that he did so, desiring me to inform him of what was going on at Court, and how it fared with me and my brother. My brother was in Champagne and the King my husband in Gascony, and there had been no communication betwixt them, though they were on terms of friendship.

I received this letter during my imprisonment, and it gave me great comfort under that situation. Although my guards had strict orders not to permit me to set pen to paper, yet, as necessity is said to be the mother of invention, I found means to write many letters to him. Some few days after I had been put under arrest, my brother had intelligence of it, which chagrined him so much that, had not the love of his country prevailed with him, the effects of his resentment would have been shown in a cruel civil war, to which purpose he had a sufficient force entirely at his devotion. He was, however, withheld by his patriotism, and contented himself with writing to the Queen my mother, informing her that, if I was thus treated, he should be driven upon some desperate measure. She, fearing the consequence of an open rupture, and dreading lest, if blows were once struck, she should be deprived of the power of bringing about a reconciliation betwixt the brothers, represented the consequences to the King, and found him well disposed to lend an ear to her reasons, as his anger was now cooled by the apprehensions of being attacked in Gascony, Dauphiny, Languedoc, and Poitou, with all the strength of the Huguenots under the King my husband. Besides the many strong places held by the Huguenots, my brother had an army with him in Champagne, composed chiefly of nobility, the bravest and best in France. The King found, since my brother's departure, that he could not, either by threats or rewards, induce a single person among the princes and great lords to act against him, so much did every one fear to intermeddle in this quarrel, which they considered as of a family nature; and after having maturely reflected on his situation, he acquiesced in my mother's opinion, and begged her to fall upon some means of reconciliation. She thereupon proposed going to my brother and taking me with her. To the measure of taking me, the King had an objection, as he considered me as the hostage for my husband and brother. She then agreed to leave me behind, and set off without my knowledge of the matter. At their interview, my brother represented to the Queen my mother that he could not but be greatly dissatisfied with the King after the many mortifications he had received at Court; that the cruelty and injustice of confining me hurt him equally as if done to himself; observing, moreover, that, as if my arrest were not a sufficient mortification, poor Torigni must be made to suffer; and concluding with the declaration of his firm resolution not to listen to any terms of peace until I was restored to my liberty, and reparation made me for the indignity I had sustained. The Queen my mother being unable to obtain any other answer, returned to Court and acquainted the King with my brother's determination. Her advice was to go back again with me, for going without me, she said, would answer very little purpose; and if I went with her in disgust, it would do more harm than good. Besides, there was reason to fear, in that case, I should insist upon going to my husband. "In short," says she, "my daughter's guard must be removed, and she must be satisfied in the best way we can."

The King agreed to follow her advice, and was now, on a sudden, as eager to reconcile matters betwixt us as she was herself. Hereupon I was sent for, and when I came to her, she informed me that she had paved the way for peace; that it was for the good of the State, which she was sensible I must be as desirous to promote as my brother; that she had it now in her power to make a peace which would be as satisfactory as my brother could desire, and would put us entirely out of the reach of Le Guast's machinations, or those of any one else who might have an influence over the King's mind. She observed that, by assisting her to procure a good understanding betwixt the King and my brother, I should relieve her from that cruel disquietude under which she at present laboured, as, should things come to an open rupture, she could not but be grieved, whichever party prevailed, as they were both her sons. She therefore expressed her hopes that I would forget the injuries I had received, and dispose myself to concur in a peace, rather than join in any plan of revenge. She assured me that the King was sorry for what had happened; that he had even expressed his regret to her with tears in his eyes, and had declared that he was ready to give me every satisfaction. I replied that I was willing to sacrifice everything for the good of my brothers and of the State; that I wished for nothing so much as peace, and that I would exert myself to the utmost to bring it about.

As I uttered these words, the King came into the closet, and, with a number of fine speeches, endeavoured to soften my resentment and to recover my friendship, to which I made such returns as might show him I harboured no ill-will for the injuries I had received. I was induced to such behaviour rather out of contempt, and because it was good policy to let the King go away satisfied with me.

Besides, I had found a secret pleasure, during my confinement, from the perusal of good books, to which I had given myself up with a delight I never before experienced. I consider this as an obligation I owe to fortune, or, rather, to Divine Providence, in order to prepare me, by such efficacious means, to bear up against the misfortunes and calamities that awaited me. By tracing nature in the universal book which is opened to all mankind, I was led to the knowledge of the Divine Author. Science conducts us, step by step, through the whole range of creation, until we arrive, at length, at God. Misfortune prompts us to summon our utmost strength to oppose grief and recover tranquillity, until at length we find a powerful aid in the knowledge and love of God, whilst prosperity hurries us away until we are overwhelmed by our passions. My captivity and its consequent solitude afforded me the double advantage of exciting a passion for study, and an inclination for devotion, advantages I had never experienced during the vanities and splendour of my prosperity.

As I have already observed, the King, discovering in me no signs of discontent, informed me that the Queen my mother was going into Champagne to have an interview with my brother, in order to bring about a peace, and begged me to accompany her thither and to use my best endeavours to forward his views, as he knew my brother was always well disposed to follow my counsel; and he concluded with saying that the peace, when accomplished, he should ever consider as being due to my good offices, and should esteem himself obliged to me for it. I promised to exert myself in so good a work, which I plainly perceived was both for my brother's advantage and the benefit of the State.

The Queen my mother and I set off for Sens the next day. The conference was agreed to be held in a gentleman's chateau, at a distance of about a league from that place. My brother was waiting for us, accompanied by a small body of troops and the principal Catholic noblemen and princes of his army. Amongst these were the Duc Casimir and Colonel Poux, who had brought him six thousand German horse, raised by the Huguenots, they having joined my brother, as the King my husband and he acted in conjunction.

The treaty was continued for several days, the conditions of peace requiring much discussion, especially such articles of it as related to religion. With respect to these, when at length agreed upon, they were too much to the advantage of the Huguenots, as it appeared afterwards, to be kept; but the Queen my mother gave in to them, in order to have a peace, and that the German cavalry before mentioned might be disbanded. She was, moreover, desirous to get my brother out of the hands of the Huguenots; and he was himself as willing to leave them, being always a very good Catholic, and joining the Huguenots only through necessity. One condition of the peace was, that my brother should have a suitable establishment. My brother likewise stipulated for me, that my marriage portion should be assigned in lands, and M. de Beauvais, a commissioner on his part, insisted much upon it. My mother, however, opposed it, and persuaded me to join her in it, assuring me that I should obtain from the King all I could require. Thereupon I begged I might not be included in the articles of peace, observing that I would rather owe whatever I was to receive to the particular favour of the King and the Queen my mother, and should, besides, consider it as more secure when obtained by such means.

The peace being thus concluded and ratified on both sides, the Queen my mother prepared to return. At this instant I received letters from the King my husband, in which he expressed a great desire to see me, begging me, as soon as peace was agreed on, to ask leave to go to him. I communicated my husband's wish to the Queen my mother, and added my own entreaties. She expressed herself greatly averse to such a measure, and used every argument to set me against it. She observed that, when I refused her proposal of a divorce after St. Bartholomew's Day, she gave way to my refusal, and commended me for it, because my husband was then converted to the Catholic religion; but now that he had abjured Catholicism, and was turned Huguenot again, she could not give her consent that I should go to him. When I still insisted upon going, she burst into a flood of tears, and said, if I did not return with her, it would prove her ruin; that the King would believe it was her doing; that she had promised to bring me back with her; and that, when my brother returned to Court, which would be soon, she would give her consent.

We now returned to Paris, and found the King well satisfied that we had made a peace; though not, however, pleased with the articles concluded in favour of the Huguenots. He therefore resolved within himself, as soon as my brother should return to Court, to find some pretext for renewing the war. These advantageous conditions were, indeed, only granted the Huguenots to get my brother out of their hands, who was detained near two months, being employed in disbanding his German horse and the rest of his army.

ETEXT EDITOR'S BOOKMARKS:

Adversity is solitary, while prosperity dwells in a crowd Comeliness of his person, which at all times pleads powerfully Everything in the world bore a double aspect Hearsay liable to be influenced by ignorance or malice Hopes they (enemies) should hereafter become our friends I should praise you more had you praised me less It is the usual frailty of our sex to be fond of flattery Mistrust is the sure forerunner of hatred Necessity is said to be the mother of invention Never approached any other man near enough to know a difference Not to repose too much confidence in our friends Prefer truth to embellishment Rather out of contempt, and because it was good policy The Massacre of St. Bartholomew's Day To embellish my story I have neither leisure nor ability Troubles might not be lasting Young girls seldom take much notice of children

www.bookjungle.com *email: sales@bookjungle.com fax: 630-214-0564 mail: Book Jungle PO Box 2226 Champaign, IL 61825*

The Codes Of Hammurabi And Moses
W. W. Davies

The discovery of the Hammurabi Code is one of the greatest achievements of archaeology, and is of paramount interest, not only to the student of the Bible, but also to all those interested in ancient history...

Religion **ISBN:** *1-59462-338-4* Pages:132 MSRP $12.95 QTY

The Theory of Moral Sentiments
Adam Smith

This work from 1749. contains original theories of conscience amd moral judgment and it is the foundation for systemof morals.

Philosophy **ISBN:** *1-59462-777-0* Pages:536 MSRP $19.95 QTY

Jessica's First Prayer
Hesba Stretton

In a screened and secluded corner of one of the many railway-bridges which span the streets of London there could be seen a few years ago, from five o'clock every morning until half past eight, a tidily set-out coffee-stall, consisting of a trestle and board, upon which stood two large tin cans, with a small fire of charcoal burning under each so as to keep the coffee boiling during the early hours of the morning when the work-people were thronging into the city on their way to their daily toil...

Childrens **ISBN:** *1-59462-373-2* Pages:84 MSRP $9.95 QTY

My Life and Work
Henry Ford

Henry Ford revolutionized the world with his implementation of mass production for the Model T automobile. Gain valuable business insight into his life and work with his own auto-biography... "We have only started on our development of our country we have not as yet, with all our talk of wonderful progress, done more than scratch the surface. The progress has been wonderful enough but..."

Biographies/ **ISBN:** *1-59462-198-5* Pages:300 MSRP $21.95

www.bookjungle.com email: sales@bookjungle.com fax: 630-214-0564 mail: Book Jungle PO Box 2226 Champaign, IL 61825

The Art of Cross-Examination
Francis Wellman

QTY

I presume it is the experience of every author, after his first book is published upon an important subject, to be almost overwhelmed with a wealth of ideas and illustrations which could readily have been included in his book, and which to his own mind, at least, seem to make a second edition inevitable. Such certainly was the case with me; and when the first edition had reached its sixth impression in five months, I rejoiced to learn that it seemed to my publishers that the book had met with a sufficiently favorable reception to justify a second and considerably enlarged edition. ..

Reference   ISBN: *1-59462-647-2*   Pages: 412   MSRP $19.95

On the Duty of Civil Disobedience
Henry David Thoreau

QTY

Thoreau wrote his famous essay, On the Duty of Civil Disobedience, as a protest against an unjust but popular war and the immoral but popular institution of slave-owning. He did more than write—he declined to pay his taxes, and was hauled off to gaol in consequence. Who can say how much this refusal of his hastened the end of the war and of slavery ?

Law   ISBN: *1-59462-747-9*   Pages: 48   MSRP $7.45

Dream Psychology Psychoanalysis for Beginners
Sigmund Freud

QTY

Sigmund Freud, born Sigismund Schlomo Freud (May 6, 1856 - September 23, 1939), was a Jewish-Austrian neurologist and psychiatrist who co-founded the psychoanalytic school of psychology. Freud is best known for his theories of the unconscious mind, especially involving the mechanism of repression; his redefinition of sexual desire as mobile and directed towards a wide variety of objects; and his therapeutic techniques, especially his understanding of transference in the therapeutic relationship and the presumed value of dreams as sources of insight into unconscious desires.

Psychology   ISBN: *1-59462-905-6*   Pages: 196   MSRP $15.45

The Miracle of Right Thought
Orison Swett Marden

QTY

Believe with all of your heart that you will do what you were made to do. When the mind has once formed the habit of holding cheerful, happy, prosperous pictures, it will not be easy to form the opposite habit. It does not matter how improbable or how far away this realization may see, or how dark the prospects may be, if we visualize them as best we can, as vividly as possible, hold tenaciously to them and vigorously struggle to attain them, they will gradually become actualized, realized in the life. But a desire, a longing without endeavor, a yearning abandoned or held indifferently will vanish without realization.

Self Help   ISBN: *1-59462-644-8*   Pages: 360   MSRP $25.45

www.bookjungle.com email: sales@bookjungle.com fax: 630-214-0564 mail: Book Jungle PO Box 2226 Champaign, IL 61825

QTY

	Title	ISBN	Price
☐	**The Rosicrucian Cosmo-Conception Mystic Christianity** by *Max Heindel*	ISBN: *1-59462-188-8*	**$38.95**
	The Rosicrucian Cosmo-conception is not dogmatic, neither does it appeal to any other authority than the reason of the student. It is: not controversial, but is: sent forth in the, hope that it may help to clear...		*New Age/Religion Pages 646*
☐	**Abandonment To Divine Providence** by *Jean-Pierre de Caussade*	ISBN: *1-59462-228-0*	**$25.95**
	"The Rev. Jean Pierre de Caussade was one of the most remarkable spiritual writers of the Society of Jesus in France in the 18th Century. His death took place at Toulouse in 1751. His works have gone through many editions and have been republished...		*Inspirational/Religion Pages 400*
☐	**Mental Chemistry** by *Charles Haanel*	ISBN: *1-59462-192-6*	**$23.95**
	Mental Chemistry allows the change of material conditions by combining and appropriately utilizing the power of the mind. Much like applied chemistry creates something new and unique out of careful combinations of chemicals the mastery of mental chemistry...		*New Age Pages 354*
☐	**The Letters of Robert Browning and Elizabeth Barret Barrett 1845-1846 vol II** by *Robert Browning* and *Elizabeth Barrett*	ISBN: *1-59462-193-4*	**$35.95**
			Biographies Pages 596
☐	**Gleanings In Genesis (volume I)** by *Arthur W. Pink*	ISBN: *1-59462-130-6*	**$27.45**
	Appropriately has Genesis been termed "the seed plot of the Bible" for in it we have, in germ form, almost all of the great doctrines which are afterwards fully developed in the books of Scripture which follow...		*Religion/Inspirational Pages 420*
☐	**The Master Key** by *L. W. de Laurence*	ISBN: *1-59462-001-6*	**$30.95**
	In no branch of human knowledge has there been a more lively increase of the spirit of research during the past few years than in the study of Psychology, Concentration and Mental Discipline. The requests for authentic lessons in Thought Control, Mental Discipline and...		*New Age/Business Pages 422*
☐	**The Lesser Key Of Solomon Goetia** by *L. W. de Laurence*	ISBN: *1-59462-092-X*	**$9.95**
	This translation of the first book of the "Lernegton" which is now for the first time made accessible to students of Talismanic Magic was done, after careful collation and edition, from numerous Ancient Manuscripts in Hebrew, Latin, and French...		*New Age/Occult Pages 92*
☐	**Rubaiyat Of Omar Khayyam** by *Edward Fitzgerald*	ISBN:*1-59462-332-5*	**$13.95**
	Edward Fitzgerald, whom the world has already learned, in spite of his own efforts to remain within the shadow of anonymity, to look upon as one of the rarest poets of the century, was born at Bredfield, in Suffolk, on the 31st of March, 1809. He was the third son of John Purcell...		*Music Pages 172*
☐	**Ancient Law** by *Henry Maine*	ISBN: *1-59462-128-4*	**$29.95**
	The chief object of the following pages is to indicate some of the earliest ideas of mankind, as they are reflected in Ancient Law, and to point out the relation of those ideas to modern thought.		*Religion/History Pages 452*
☐	**Far-Away Stories** by *William J. Locke*	ISBN: *1-59462-129-2*	**$19.45**
	"Good wine needs no bush, but a collection of mixed vintages does. And this book is just such a collection. Some of the stories I do not want to remain buried for ever in the museum files of dead magazine-numbers an author's not unpardonable vanity..."		*Fiction Pages 272*
☐	**Life of David Crockett** by *David Crockett*	ISBN: *1-59462-250-7*	**$27.45**
	"Colonel David Crockett was one of the most remarkable men of the times in which he lived. Born in humble life, but gifted with a strong will, an indomitable courage, and unremitting perseverance...		*Biographies/New Age Pages 424*
☐	**Lip-Reading** by *Edward Nitchie*	ISBN: *1-59462-206-X*	**$25.95**
	Edward B. Nitchie, founder of the New York School for the Hard of Hearing, now the Nitchie School of Lip-Reading, Inc, wrote "LIP-READING Principles and Practice". The development and perfecting of this meritorious work on lip-reading was an undertaking...		*How-to Pages 400*
☐	**A Handbook of Suggestive Therapeutics, Applied Hypnotism, Psychic Science** by *Henry Munro*	ISBN: *1-59462-214-0*	**$24.95**
			Health/New Age/Health/Self-help Pages 376
☐	**A Doll's House: and Two Other Plays** by *Henrik Ibsen*	ISBN: *1-59462-112-8*	**$19.95**
	Henrik Ibsen created this classic when in revolutionary 1848 Rome. Introducing some striking concepts in playwriting for the realist genre, this play has been studied the world over.		*Fiction/Classics/Plays 308*
☐	**The Light of Asia** by *sir Edwin Arnold*	ISBN: *1-59462-204-3*	**$13.95**
	In this poetic masterpiece, Edwin Arnold describes the life and teachings of Buddha. The man who was to become known as Buddha to the world was born as Prince Gautama of India but he rejected the worldly riches and abandoned the reigns of power when...		*Religion/History/Biographies Pages 170*
☐	**The Complete Works of Guy de Maupassant** by *Guy de Maupassant*	ISBN: *1-59462-157-8*	**$16.95**
	"For days and days, nights and nights, I had dreamed of that first kiss which was to consecrate our engagement, and I knew not on what spot I should put my lips..."		*Fiction/Classics Pages 240*
☐	**The Art of Cross-Examination** by *Francis L. Wellman*	ISBN: *1-59462-309-0*	**$26.95**
	Written by a renowned trial lawyer, Wellman imparts his experience and uses case studies to explain how to use psychology to extract desired information through questioning.		*How-to/Science/Reference Pages 408*
☐	**Answered or Unanswered?** by *Louisa Vaughan*	ISBN: *1-59462-248-5*	**$10.95**
	Miracles of Faith in China		*Religion Pages 112*
☐	**The Edinburgh Lectures on Mental Science (1909)** by *Thomas*	ISBN: *1-59462-008-3*	**$11.95**
	This book contains the substance of a course of lectures recently given by the writer in the Queen Street Hall, Edinburgh. Its purpose is to indicate the Natural Principles governing the relation between Mental Action and Material Conditions...		*New Age/Psychology Pages 148*
☐	**Ayesha** by *H. Rider Haggard*	ISBN: *1-59462-301-5*	**$24.95**
	Verily and indeed it is the unexpected that happens! Probably if there was one person upon the earth from whom the Editor of this, and of a certain previous history, did not expect to hear again...		*Classics Pages 380*
☐	**Ayala's Angel** by *Anthony Trollope*	ISBN: *1-59462-352-X*	**$29.95**
	The two girls were both pretty, but Lucy who was twenty-one who supposed to be simple and comparatively unattractive, whereas Ayala was credited, as her Bombwhat romantic name might show, with poetic charm and a taste for romance. Ayala when her father died was nineteen...		*Fiction Pages 484*
☐	**The American Commonwealth** by *James Bryce*	ISBN: *1-59462-286-8*	**$34.45**
	An interpretation of American democratic political theory. It examines political mechanics and society from the perspective of Scotsman James Bryce		*Politics Pages 572*
☐	**Stories of the Pilgrims** by *Margaret P. Pumphrey*	ISBN: *1-59462-116-0*	**$17.95**
	This book explores pilgrims religious oppression in England as well as their escape to Holland and eventual crossing to America on the Mayflower, and their early days in New England...		*History Pages 268*

www.bookjungle.com *email:* sales@bookjungle.com *fax:* 630-214-0564 *mail:* Book Jungle PO Box 2226 Champaign, IL 61825

QTY

The Fasting Cure *by Sinclair Upton*   ISBN: *1-59462-222-1*   **$13.95**
In the Cosmopolitan Magazine for May, 1910, and in the Contemporary Review (London) for April, 1910, I published an article dealing with my experiences in fasting. I have written a great many magazine articles, but never one which attracted so much attention...   *New Age/Self Help/Health Pages 164*

Hebrew Astrology *by Sepharial*   ISBN: *1-59462-308-2*   **$13.45**
In these days of advanced thinking it is a matter of common observation that we have left many of the old landmarks behind and that we are now pressing forward to greater heights and to a wider horizon than that which represented the mind-content of our progenitors...   *Astrology Pages 144*

Thought Vibration or The Law of Attraction in the Thought World   ISBN: *1-59462-127-6*   **$12.95**
by William Walker Atkinson   *Psychology/Religion Pages 144*

Optimism *by Helen Keller*   ISBN: *1-59462-108-X*   **$15.95**
Helen Keller was blind, deaf, and mute since 19 months old, yet famously learned how to overcome these handicaps, communicate with the world, and spread her lectures promoting optimism. An inspiring read for everyone...   *Biographies/Inspirational Pages 84*

Sara Crewe *by Frances Burnett*   ISBN: *1-59462-360-0*   **$9.45**
In the first place, Miss Minchin lived in London. Her home was a large, dull, tall one, in a large, dull square, where all the houses were alike, and all the sparrows were alike, and where all the door-knockers made the same heavy sound...   *Childrens/Classic Pages 88*

The Autobiography of Benjamin Franklin *by Benjamin Franklin*   ISBN: *1-59462-135-7*   **$24.95**
The Autobiography of Benjamin Franklin has probably been more extensively read than any other American historical work, and no other book of its kind has had such ups and downs of fortune. Franklin lived for many years in England, where he was agent...   *Biographies/History Pages 332*

Name	
Email	
Telephone	
Address	
City, State ZIP	

☐ Credit Card   ☐ Check / Money Order

Credit Card Number	
Expiration Date	
Signature	

Please Mail to: Book Jungle
                    PO Box 2226
                    Champaign, IL 61825
or Fax to: 630-214-0564

ORDERING INFORMATION

web: *www.bookjungle.com*
email: *sales@bookjungle.com*
fax: *630-214-0564*
mail: *Book Jungle PO Box 2226 Champaign, IL 61825*
or PayPal *to sales@bookjungle.com*

Please contact us for bulk discounts

DIRECT-ORDER TERMS

**20% Discount if You Order
Two or More Books**
Free Domestic Shipping!
Accepted: Master Card, Visa,
Discover, American Express

www.ingramcontent.com/pod-product-compliance
Lightning Source LLC
Chambersburg PA
CBHW081327040426
42453CB00013B/2324